SPIRITUAL COUNSEL

and

LETTERS

of

BARON FRIEDRICH VON HÜGEL

by Douglas V. Steere:

DIMENSIONS OF PRAYER *(1962)*

DOORS INTO LIFE Through Five Devotional Classics *(1948)*

ON BEGINNING FROM WITHIN and ON LISTENING TO
ANOTHER *(one volume edition, 1964)*

PRAYER AND WORSHIP *(1937)*

TIME TO SPARE *(1949)*

WORK AND CONTEMPLATION *(1957)*

translated by Douglas V. Steere:

Søren Kierkegaard: PURITY OF HEART *(1938)*

SPIRITUAL COUNSEL
and
LETTERS
of
BARON FRIEDRICH VON HÜGEL

Edited with an Introductory Essay

by

Douglas V. Steere

HARPER & ROW

PUBLISHERS

New York and Evanston

CONTENTS

Preface

I ONCE asked my father when he would advise me to prune my apple trees. His answer was, 'Whenever your saw is sharp.' A similar answer might be given to the query as to when von Hügel's writings would make suitable religious reading : whenever you hunger or thirst after a more authentic religious life. For there is no dating von Hügel in his spiritual counsels. In them, he is speaking a universal word to a universal need. He did, as his niece suggests, quarry great chunks out of himself and his experience of God and shared them with others, and the following collection is taken from the rough granite that he left us as his legacy. It speaks as livingly to us today as when it was written in the first quarter of this century when this great mind helped to shape the best in Anglo-Saxon religious thought.

The *Selected Letters* from which the majority of the letters published here were taken have not to my knowledge been re-printed since 1933, so that they have become inaccessible to most people who do not have access to a scholarly library. Since 1950 there has appeared not only Michael de la Bedoyère's biography of von Hügel in which he has had access to the von Hügel family papers that had never before been available, but there has also come the *Life of Evelyn Underhill* by Lucy Menzies and Margaret Cropper in which, for the first time, the full set of von Hügel's letters to Mrs Stuart Moore (E.U.) were published. These two events, plus the material now in the British Museum, have encouraged me to venture this set of selections of the letters and counsels in order that this generation can come freely into touch with this monumental religious spirit.

The accent in these selections has been to set forth the letters and the passages from von Hügel's writings that speak of the life of the spirit, and the term 'spiritual' has been broadly interpreted. As a matter of fact, much of the heart of his teaching is contained in this group of selections. For the reader who is in search of personal spiritual nurture, the introductory essay and Chapters III-V and Chapter IX may have particular interest. For the seekers after the broad frames within which an authentic religion must move, and who know that they are keeping company with one whom his contemporaries regarded as the ranking religious interpreter of his generation, Chapters VI-VIII will be of special concern. Von Hügel is not a 'read as you run' writer. Sentences have to be pondered and their substance absorbed. At times there is a Teutonic inclusiveness about them which will exasperate. But the patience exerted will have a rich reward.

I should like to acknowledge the generous permissions of the following publishers for my use of letters and passages from books which they have published. The source of each piece of material used is indicated immediately after it in this book by the abbreviations which precede the list of sources shown below :

J. M. Dent & Sons Ltd, London and E. P. Dutton Co., New York

EA—*Essays and Addresses on the Philosophy of Religion,* Vol. I (1921)

EA 2—*Essays and Addresses on the Philosophy of Religion,* Vol. II (1926)

RG—*The Reality of God* (1930)

ME 1—*The Mystical Element of Religion as Studied in St Catherine of Genoa and her Friends,* Vol I (1908)

ME 2—*The Mystical Element of Religion as Studied in St Catherine of Genoa and her Friends,* Vol II (1908)

SL—*Selected Letters 1896–1924* (ed. with a memoir by Bernard Holland, 1927)

LTN—*Letters of Baron Friedrich von Hügel to a Niece* (ed. with an introduction by Gwendolyn Green, 1929)

J. M. Dent & Sons Ltd, London

VHT—M. D. Petre : *Von Hügel and Tyrell* (1937)

B—Michael de la Bedoyère. *The Life of Baron von Hügel* (1951)

GS—*The German Soul* (1916)

T. & T. Clark, Edinburgh

EL—Baron von Hügel : *Eternal Life* (1913)

Longmans, Green & Co. Ltd, London and Harper & Row, Publishers Inc., New York

Margaret Cropper : *The Life of Evelyn Underhill* (1957)

I should also like to thank Margaret Bro for her admirable suggestions for improving the style of the introductory essay; my daughter, Helen Steere, for her vigilant reading of the manuscript and her helpful suggestions; Mildred Hargreaves for another manuscript so carefully prepared for the publisher; and my wife for the continuous help on all fronts in managing this little book.

DOUGLAS V. STEERE

Haverford, Pa.
January 15, 1962

Baron von Hügel as a Spiritual Director

BARON FRIEDRICH von Hügel was in himself a kind of European ecumenical movement. He was born in 1852 in Florence, the eldest child of a late marriage between a mature Austrian diplomat, Baron Karl von Hügel who was serving as Austrian Ambassador to the court of Tuscany, and a beautiful young Scottish girl not yet twenty, who was the daughter of General Farquharson. After seven years of service in Italy, his father became Ambassador to Belgium and the son spent the next seven years in a French-Flemish civilization with his education largely directed by two Germans, one a Catholic diplomat and historian, and the other a Protestant pastor. Upon his father's retirement, the family moved to Torquay in England where a Quaker, William Pengelly, opened to him the world of geology. As a result of this remarkable education, von Hügel for the rest of his life was not only completely at home in German, Italian, French and English, to say nothing of Latin, Greek, and Hebrew, but as a Roman Catholic he was able to speak with great understanding to the Protestant mind of his generation.

When he was twenty-one, Friedrich von Hügel married Lady Mary, the daughter of Sidney Herbert, a member of Gladstone's Cabinet, and three daughters were born to them. von Hügel inherited a small income from his father, which with modest living was enough to meet his family's needs. A generous slice of it was always reserved for charity. This situation set him free to give himself to the life of the scholar and counselor without the dispersion of an outside vocation.

Apart from some nine winters spent in Rome where he was in the closest contact with Vatican scholars and officials, he lived his whole adult life in England and his books were all written in English. Having inherited from his father his title as a Baron of the Holy Roman Empire, he remained an Austrian citizen until the outbreak of the first World War.

Von Hügel first made his scholarly reputation through scientific biblical papers, but the enormous theological and philosophical learning which he assembled quietly over thirty years in his capacity as a private scholar was no secret to the best British men of letters who sat with him, first in the Synthetic Society

1

and later in what became almost his personal passion, the London Society for the Study of Religion. It would be hard to overestimate what these two intellectual clubs meant to the mutual stimulation of the members in their work. Just as, a generation before, the best German spiritual culture was hammered out and nurtured in the passionate weekly or fortnightly meetings in some café around a Martin Buber in Frankfurt or a Theodore Haecker in Munich, so these London gatherings in their lively although somewhat more moderate exchanges furnished a climate of growth that von Hügel and his distinguished comrades cherished.

'Baron von Hügel was our Greatest Theologian . . .'

When his great two-volume *Mystical Element of Religion* on which he had worked for twelve years finally appeared in 1908, von Hügel, like Kant at the appearance of the first *Critique*, was in his middle fifties. From this time until his death in 1925, von Hügel became acknowledged in Britain as doyen of the theological and religious writers of his generation. This reputation was further confirmed by the appearance in 1913 of his *Eternal Life* and in 1921 of the first volume of his *Essays and Addresses on the Philosophy of Religion*. The second series of *Essays and Addresses*, the *Selected Letters*, and *The Reality of God* were published posthumously and these went even further in underlining von Hügel's standing in his generation. Dean William Inge, who was not especially given to fulsome praise, once wrote of him, 'Baron von Hügel was our greatest theologian and the ablest apologist for Christianity in our time'.

Unlike John Henry Newman, von Hügel as a Roman Catholic layman held no official position in the Church. Yet apart from Newman, in the century from 1825-1925, it would be hard to find a figure in Britain to compare with von Hügel either in stature or in influence on Protestant and Catholic alike. He numbered his scholarly friends from both confessions and from both Britain and the continent, and his vast correspondence was written freely by hand in French, German, Italian, or English to suit the convenience of the receiver. In Germany there were Protestants like Troeltsch and Holtzmann; in France Catholic men of letters like Loisy, Blondel, Brémond and Laberthonnièrre; in Italy, Duschène, Murri and Fogazzaro; in Sweden, Archbishop Söderblom. In Britain itself he exerted a profound personal influence on men and women like George Tyrrell, Maude Petre, C. C. J. Webb, A. E. Taylor, Norman Kemp Smith, Evelyn Underhill, Dean Inge, and Claude Montefiore, to name only a few.

This rare and astonishing gift for friendship, and for the kind of friendship that engages with the ideas of another, often took the form of letters to a writer whom von Hügel had 'discovered' in which he expressed his deep indebtedness for some freshly expressed insight. No one will ever know what these letters of discriminating encouragement meant to the recipients. Left very deaf by a bout of typhus fever in his early manhood, letters were easier for him to manage than personal visits, but these latter were far from excluded, and at his home in London he was host to a wide range of Christian seekers.

His Own Debt to Spiritual Guides

He felt that in any spiritual counsel he could share, he was only repaying in a small way what had been lavished on him at two great crises in his life, one in late adolescence and another at a kind of spiritual climacteric at the age of forty, by spiritual guides of great wisdom. These men had helped him to move on into a life of increasing self-abandonment to God within the life and station in which he stood.

In 1910 he wrote a letter to Emelia Fogelklou, a Swedish Quaker friend of mine, telling her what he owed to these two men:

My own conversion came through, or on the occasion of, my first sacramental confession when a precocious, wholesome, much-complicated soul of (turned) fifteen. It was deepened appreciably when at eighteen by the, to me, utterly unforgettable example, silent influence, and definite teaching of a mystically minded but scholastically trained Dutch Dominican [Father Raymond Hocking] in Vienna when I was sickening with typhus fever, when my father had just died, and when 'the world' which till then had looked so brilliant to me, turned out so distant, cold, shallow. And the final depth attained so far was mediated for me at forty. I felt at the time and feel still that it came straight from God, yet on the occasion of and by the help of man—by a physically suffering, spiritually aboundingly helpful, mystical saint, a French secular priest [Abbé Huvelin] dead now since only a year.[1]

Ten years later, he passed on to his niece Gwendolyn Greene, a flash of what the first guide had taught him.

When at eighteen, I made up my mind to go into moral and religious training, the great soul and mind who took me in hand—a noble Dominican—warned me—'you want to grow in virtue, to serve God, to love Christ? Well, you will grow in and attain these things if you will make them a slow and sure, an utterly real, mountain-step plod and ascent, willing to have to camp for weeks in spiritual desolation, darkness and emptiness at different stages in your march and growth. All demand for constant light, all attempt at eliminating or mini- mizing the cross and trial, is so much soft folly and puerile trifling.' And what Father Hocking taught me as to spirituality is of course, also true, in its way, of all study worthy of the name.[2]

In his *Eternal Life*, von Hügel speaks of what the second guide, the Abbé Huvelin, had taught him about the service of one soul to another:

There is before my mind with all the vividness resulting from direct personal intercourse and deep spiritual obligations, the figure of the Abbé Huvelin ... a gentleman by birth and breeding, a distinguished Hellenist, a man of exquisitely pierc- ing, humorous mind, he could readily have become a great editor or interpreter of Greek philosophical or patristic texts, or a remarkable Church historian. But this deep and heroic personality deliberately preferred 'to write in souls', whilst oc- cupying, during thirty-five years, a supernumerary, unpaid post in a large Parisian parish. There, suffering from gout in the eyes and brain, and usually lying prone in a darkened room, he served souls with the supreme authority of self- oblivious love, and brought light and purity and peace to countless troubled, sorrowing or sinful souls ... In the *Confer- ences on Some of the Spiritual Guides of the Seventeenth Cen-*

1. From a copy of the original letter supplied by Emelia Fogelklou Norlind.
2. *Selected Letters of Friedrich von Hügel*, ed. by Bernard Holland. London: Dent, 1927, p. 266.

tury, Huvelin once declared, 'God who might have created us directly, employs, for this work, our parents, to whom He joins us by the tenderest ties. He could also save us directly, but He saves us, in fact, by means of certain souls, which have received the spiritual life before ourselves, and which communicate it to us, because they love us.'[3]

A Theology of Spiritual Guidance

It is quite impossible to understand von Hügel and his service to his generation without giving full weight to the ideal which these men had visited upon his mind and to the vision which they had opened to him about his own ultimate vocation. It is my own personal conviction that this service of spiritual counsel on the part of von Hügel was not, as some of his family regarded it, an incidental avocation or an intrusion that sapped away much energy and attention from his theological and philosophical writing. On the contrary, this service of spiritual counseling was the central axis that even set the frames for his intellectual contribution. For that reason, when we come at last to assess the significance of the contribution of this religious giant, I believe that it will be as a guide and encourager of souls that he will be chiefly remembered.

Von Hügel's philosophical and theological contributions are of immense suggestiveness. His monumental study of *The Mystical Element of Religion* is in its depth without parallel in our century. In the course of developing a highly tenable theory of religious realism in *Eternal Life,* in *The Reality of God* and, in a more casual way, in his two volumes of *Essays and Addresses on the Philosophy of Religion,* he recovered for the Anglo-Saxon religious world the dimension of transcendence in the Christian faith and thus did much to correct a current strain of subjectively-tilted psychologism in liberal religion. In Britain, at least, this also did much to spare it from the long and debilitating hang-over that would almost certainly have followed if British religion had been compelled to receive this corrective by means of a rebottled import of continental Barthianism. I remember Canon Streeter remarking one day how thankful he was that British religion had received this accent on the transcendent from von Hügel instead of Barth, and adding wryly, 'We shall one day have so much less to unlearn'.

3. *Eternal Life.* Edinburgh: T. & T. Clark, 1912, pp. 374–376.

Finally von Hügel's witness to the significance of corporate worship and to the historical and institutional side of religion came with peculiar timeliness and weight to a generation of liberal free churchmen whose offerings leaned in the direction of moralistic preaching and who regarded the Church primarily as a convenient 'pulpit' from which to speak.

There needs to be no minimizing of the significance of these theological and philosophical thrusts of Baron von Hügel for the life of our time, when it is nevertheless asserted that the impact of his writing will in the long run be felt in its genius as a spiritual witness to the encompassing reality of God and to its power in encouraging the nurture which men and women require in order to grow in their awareness of that encompassment and to respond appropriately to it. It is striking what confirmation of this assessment one gets as he notes how quaintly von Hügel's books are studded with passages that do not belong in the precise and measured assaying of a religious problem. In the least likely places in his writings, there flames forth a burst of witness or an admonition that seems only to be focused on guidance of the spiritual life of the reader.

Adoration and Religious Realism

His insistence in personal counsel, for example, that religion is adoration, and that any approach to religion that ignores the adoration of God is 'like a triangle with one side left out' gives the clue to a major factor in his rejection of idealism in favor of a form of religious realism. This philosophical scaffolding of realism, of an admission that there is a vast givenness in God which we encounter, which we apprehend but never fully comprehend, which penetrates us, which stirs our organs to response, and yet which always preserves its abyss of mystery in the very course of quickening our souls—what is this but a description of a kind of stance by which the soul is poised and directed toward the Object of adoration? The guide of souls, knowing that a soul must adore if it is to grow into an awareness of encompassment, has sketched a rough philosophical diagram that shows how this interpretation of the soul's relationship to God sheds illumination on the act of religious growth at the same time as it provides a crude philosophical road map which serves for the other areas of life experience as well. The goal of his philosophical and theological thought is always identical. It is to give a clue to the breathing space the soul requires if it is to slip the tightly knotted bands of self-serving and move into the heroic self-spending company of the servants of God.

The Requirements of a Full Religious Ration

This same focus upon the guidance of souls is seen in von Hügel's highly plausible account of the three elements in religion that is expanded in the first eighty pages of his *Mystical Element of Religion*. Here a full and fruitful religion is described as containing a creative tension between the mystical or emotional element, the historical or institutional element, and the intellectual or scientific element. If religious practice attempts to delete or to neglect the critical scrutiny of the intellectual and scientific element of religion, it not only weighs itself down with superstitious accretions, outdated cultural patterns, and often with uncriticized ethical practices of a spurious character, but it is powerless to engage fully with the thought of the generation in which it lives in order to express to them in viable terms the truth it longs to share.

If religious practice should seek to omit or write off as 'enthusiasm' the mystical and emotional element in religion, in favor of some rigid intellectual or ethical formula or in an effort to preserve intact some set of traditional institutional forms, then the elegant heating plant stands as frigid and useless as an automatic oil furnace when a storm has cut off the current.

If in the burst of an enlightenment period, religious practice seeks to live on intellect or science alone, or in a romantic age to exist on an exclusive inward focus upon the mystical and emotional element of religion, scorning the historical element with its witness to an historical revelation and turning its back on its institutional counterpart, the Church, then once again impoverishment results and that healthy staple of sound Christian religion, a deep sense of 'creatureliness' dries up and disappears. This neglect of the historical and institutional element in religion often produces side effects, anemic aberrations in the form of synthetically fabricated intellectual and scientific religions or of the emaciated and twisted stereotypes and patterns of emotional religion, neither of which is crossed and humbled and fructified by some corporate transmission of a great normative revelation.

On a corporate scale where these personal tendencies are writ large, it is not difficult to see the thrust of von Hügel's analysis in Unitarianism where the intellectual and ethical have been to the fore, or in Quakerism where the mystical and the intellectual have been favored over the historical, or in the Roman Catholic Church where, in the modernist struggle in which von Hügel was deeply involved, the historical-institutional was being exalted over the intellectual and scientific. Yet here, at bottom, von Hügel is once again giving a formula for the guidance of souls and insisting that the full response to the encompassing reality must draw the soul to prize the fruitful tension of all three of these elements operating in it simultaneously, and that it will ignore any of them only at its peril.

The spiritual guide who will speak to the soul's real need must teach it the place of each of these elements in a full religious diet or ration. He must cultivate the inner mystical life through the practice of private and corporate prayer and worship. The spiritual guide must also meet the terrible gravity-like pull of sin in the one he is guiding by the historical revelation of God's redemptive power in Jesus Christ. In full awareness of the shortness of man's memory, he must make sure that there is no neglect of the historical and institutional element that serves as a constant reminder of man's calling and of his redemption, and which in the course of kindling in him an unlimited liability for others, enlists him as a member of a great company of the living and the dead who are involved in this redemption of the cosmos. And finally, the guide of souls must encourage the educated seeker in a deep and abiding respect for the intellectual and the scientific element and in the latter case seek even to suggest, at least in an amateur way, the practice of some objective scientific pursuit so that the purifying, other-directed discipline fo scientific objectivity may chasten and scarify the almost universal predisposition to self-absorption. All is a laying of a framework within which a guidance of individual souls may be most effectively carried out.

The Nature of Religious Truth and the Nurture of Souls

In his reaction against the arrogant finality of the stiff, hard, geometrical pattern of scholastic distinctions as applied to the deepest reality of all, it is hard once again not to see the guide of souls at work. Speaking of this scholastic tendency in the

elder Wilfred Ward's mind, in a letter which he wrote to Algar
Thorold on August 15, 1921, von Hügel declared:

I believe men's minds to be largely, perhaps all, classable
according as they act as follows: they instinctively push out
to the margins of things and there they remain restless and
dissatisfied unless and until they there perceive or think they
perceive, clear lines of demarcation. Such minds see truth,
reality of all kinds—or what they take to be such—as so many
geometrical figures: within these luminous lines all is true,
'safe', 'correct'; outside them at once begins error, 'danger', in-
correctness. Such was W. G. Ward's mind—at least as he
willed and worked that it should be. Then there are other
minds which see truth's realities as intensely luminous centres,
with a semi-illuminated outer margin, and then another and
another, till all shades off into outer darkness. Such minds are
not in the least perturbed by each having to stammer and to
stumble. When they have moved out some distance, they fall
back upon their central light. They become perturbed really,
only if and when minds of the geometrical type will force
them for the time into their own approach and apprehension.

This kind of insight and flexibility in dealing with theological
distinctions points once more to von Hügel's extraordinary
flexibility in understanding souls of very different types who all
need broadening and deepening if they are to resist the business
of a too early firming up, and yet souls each of which has a bent
that must be reckoned with and helped to bring its particular
gift to the service of truth.

Whether it is the treatment of the problem of the relation of
God to evil and suffering, or the yearning for immortality in
man, or of the experience of nature and of the ordinary responses
of the senses, of the creation of an object of art, of the achieve-
ment of a moral victory as witnessing in a preliminary way to
the continual operation upon man of a Greater than himself, the
same accent is to be seen. Without any interpolation whatever,
von Hügel's humble handling of the problem is immediately
translatable to the guidance of souls who are faced with both
the daily fabric of life and with life's extremities.

There is no intention here of suggesting that von Hügel is a
kind of religious pragmatist who is satisfied with any resolution
of a problem that will bring a smooth and swift anesthesia to an

aching heart. The younger Wilfred Ward wrote von Hügel in the early nineties that what he prized in him very especially was his refusal to oversimplify religion. Instead he presented religion in all of its stark complexity and mystery and yet as lighted up by a faith in its power to transform men and to fashion out of them a company of the highest characters that human history has ever known. It was only by helping man face what *is*, that von Hügel felt he could ever be stirred to move outward to what *ought to be* and not vice versa. Yet the bent of mind of von Hügel never leaves out of sight for a moment the object of his quest: namely to minister to the hungering souls of men.

If it should be queried whether this is not the ultimate aim of all sound theology, the answer called for would seem to be a thumping affirmative. This does not, however, wipe out either the distinction or the accent that has just been explored. For in most of what passes for theology it would only be with considerable homiletic skill that a distillate of the implications for the guidance of souls could be obtained, and there might well be elements of the theological position which when so applied to human guidance would turn out to be literally destructive of the hope of souls. The devout evangelical Christian humanism of von Hügel, on the other hand, moves back and forth between the revelation of God in the Christian tradition and the condition and needs of the soul like a weaving shuttle, and while there is no claim that he has ever presented a fully articulated system of theology, the problems he has touched upon are always approached in this fashion and his contribution to them would seem finally to be accented heavily in this direction.

Von Hügel's Qualifications as a Spiritual Director

Von Hügel had at least four signal gifts as a spiritual director. In the first instance, he was saturated with an awareness that God was at work, that he is present and operative and laying siege to every soul before, during, and after any spiritual director might come upon the scene. He loved to quote Bernard of Clairvaux on the prevenience of God where Bernard is speaking of a Cistercian monk who thought he could get into the place of prayer before God was there.

Do you awake? Well, he too is awake. If you rise in the night time, if you anticipate to your utmost your earliest awaking, you will already find Him waking, you will never anticipate His own awakeness. In such an intercourse you will always be rash if you attribute any priority, any predominant share to yourself: for He loves both more than you love, and before you love at all.[4]

Then, he knew himself what it was to be a needy one. 'People often ask me what religion is for,' he confided to his niece. 'I simply cannot get on without it. I must have it to moderate me, to water me down, to make me possible. I am so claimful, so self-occupied, so intense. I want everything my own way.'[5] Break-downs, shattering disappointments, personal suffering, long spells of dryness, these he had known at first hand, and in his extremity he had found what a firmly rooted spiritual counselor like Raymond Hocking or Huvelin could do to help bring his life back into its true focus again. Von Hügel not only bore in his own flesh the scars of past need but this was the kind of need that returned continually. 'I need Thee Every Hour' was not a sentimental hymn to von Hügel. Hence his constant personal dependence upon daily religious practice inoculated him against any underestimation of the magnitude of the resistance in men and women to the growing self-abandonment which the interior life requires. He knew, too, how swiftly a life could be impover-ished which either neglected or felt that it had passed beyond the staple remedies that have been given men for countering the relentless downward pull of the worldly adhesions of the soul.

In addition to these two qualifications, he also had a profound reverence for the differences in souls. 'Never forget the enormous variety of souls,' he warned his niece. He had experienced the costly failure of his early attempt to throw his own pattern and concerns upon his gifted elder daughter, Gertrud, and had been painfully liberated from the shriveling but widely pervasive temptation that haunts a director, that of regarding his own re-ligious experience as normative, and of seeking to shape all souls like his own. 'One is enough,' Emerson warned a teacher who sought to stamp his pupils with his own signet, and the thrust of the punster's 'One man's Mede is another man's Persian' seemed to distinguish every step in von Hügel's mature approach to spiritual guidance. He quoted with gusto the final sentence of Fredrick William Faber's lecture on Ignatius of Loyola. 'This

4. *Sermons on Canticles of Canticles*, 69:8.
5. *Letters to a Niece*, Gwendolyn Greene. London: Dent, 1928, xxv.

then, my dear brethren, is St. Ignatius' way to heaven: and thank God, it is not the only way.'[6]

To his niece Gwendolyn Greene he gave the following counsel:

> The golden rule is to help those we love to escape from us ... Souls are never mere dittos. The souls thus helped are mostly at quite different stages from our own, or they have a quite different *attrait*. We must be tolerant and patient, too, with these we can and ought to help. This difference in souls wakes us up, and makes us more sensitive and perceptive.[7]

Finally, von Hügel was himself expendable in the business of guiding souls. There seemed little or no sense of self-preservation left in him and he gave himself without reserve to those whom he believed God had sent to him for help. With at most a working capacity of only two or three hours a day, because of his frailty in the closing years of his life, with his 'brain-fag, an old friend', his extreme deafness, his frequent 'white nights' where he shared the insomnia of God, with his growing obligations for essays and addresses at important occasions that culminated in the great honor of the invitation to deliver a set of the Gifford Lectures, he still found time to lavish on persons like Gwendolyn Greene and Evelyn Underhill, the richest treasure of counsel that he could mobilize. Moreover they were continually in his prayers. 'Three times a day, I pray for you.'

He wrote to Evelyn Underhill in 1921, four years before his death:

> One little word more. Do not, I pray you, if ever you feel at all clearly that I could help you in any way—even if by only silently listening to such trouble and complications as God may send you—do not because I am busy, shrink from coming to me, or letting me come to you. We are *both* busy, so we have each the guarantee that we will not take up each other's time without good cause. But such good cause arising, it would, it will be nothing but consolation for me, if you let me help as much as ever you feel the need. I will pray my little best for you, that God may bless and keep you along this path—so safe and so sound—and which (at least in time) will

6. *Essays and Addresses* (Second Series). London: Dent, 1926, p. 232.
7. *Letters to a Niece*, Gwendolyn Greene. London: Dent, 1928, p. xxix.

bring you consolations of a depth and richness far surpassing the old ones.[8]

Without in any way contradicting what has been said above about von Hügel's humility before the ultimate mystery and uniqueness of the souls of those he guided, it is equally clear that his expendability was such that if he thought that any experience which had come to him would be helpful to another, he was not restrained for an instant by any false reticence or fear of disclosing his own personal humiliation or weakness from sharing it freely with the one he was guiding. Yet all of this was done with a delicate readiness and even positive suggestion that it be laid aside or rejected if it was not immediately helpful.

His niece wrote of this quality: 'He lived in a deep interior world where few, perhaps, can follow—giving himself to an interior life; tearing, as it were, out of himself great chunks of truth and bringing them to the surface, explaining to us what we can gather and understand.'[9] In another place, she records his own counsel to her about what to do with these 'chunks'. 'Leave out all that does not help you. Take only what you can and what helps. Wipe your feet on my old hair, if it will help you, my little old thing.'[10]

A Case Study in Spiritual Direction

Perhaps the most effective way of seeing von Hügel at work as a director of souls would be to take a specific instance and look into it carefully enough to indicate some of the characteristics of his method of approach.

In 1921, after a good deal of reflection, Evelyn Underhill (Mrs Stuart Moore) asked Friedrich von Hügel to act as a spiritual guide for her. She was in her middle forties and von Hügel was approaching seventy. She was an Anglican and von Hügel a Roman Catholic. Both were acknowledged intellectual leaders in the British religious circle of their day. She had known von Hügel for over ten years and during a part of this time had had a number of personal visits with him. She sensed that with all of his great gifts for friendship, he was not easy at the immanentist foundations of her faith nor at her interpretation of Christian

8. *Evelyn Underhill*, Margaret Cropper. New York: Harper, 1958, p. 70.
9. *Two Witnesses*, Gwendolyn Greene. London: Dent, 1930, p. 101.
10. *Letters to a Niece*, Gwendolyn Greene. London: Dent, 1928, p. x.

spiritual life in her *Mysticism* (1911) and subsequently in the row of volumes that had followed it.

It was not her first experience with a Roman Catholic spiritual guide. After a time of spiritual renewal that lifted her out of agnosticism, and before her marriage, which took place in her middle thirties, she had consulted Father Robert Hugh Benson and by 1909 had been on the point of being taken into the Roman Catholic Church. The rugged objection of her lawyer fiancé and the heavy hand of the Roman Church's anti-modernist oath that had appeared at just that point, had restrained her from taking the step.

Now in 1921, some twelve years later, she had once again had an unexpected flood of spiritual renewal. The war years had taken their spiritual toll, and had left her inwardly dispersed. Outwardly, apart from the shock of the death of her beloved friend, Ethel Barker, everything seemed coming her way. She was happily married. She had a circle of unusually intimate and devoted friends. She was secure and 'even petted', as she put it, in her professional life, and as a writer on religion she enjoyed the somewhat flattering experience of having a growing number of people who wrote to her for spiritual help. Yet this latter circumstance had, as always, its barb within it. For this growing reliance upon her for help brought with it a growing doubt in her that her spiritual foundation was strong enough even to carry her own life, let alone to nurture others. With her uncannily shrewd power of self-analysis, she had her hunch where the trouble lay. She knew that she was given to strong antipathies, and that one of them was for the institutional aspect of religion. This led to her minimizing the historical and sacramental element in religion and to a pressing of the mystical, experiential element as overwhelmingly decisive. She also knew that in her own practice of the Christian religion, any personal attachment to Christ seemed to her sentimental and unreal and she knew, too, that the theocentric approach in prayer and worship was her natural bent.

Curriculum for a School of Sanctity

Still more deeply, from her touch with the great souls of Christian history and from this utterly undeserved and unexpected surge of the forgiving love of God that had lifted her up out of the dispersion in which in the war years she had, in Augustine's words, 'turned from Thee the One and been vainly divided', she knew that she was marked for sanctity. But she knew equally well how much in her and in her extremely well-adjusted life resisted this call, how much might have to go, and that without stronger help and guidance than she could herself provide she would almost certainly sink back on the outward assurances and fail both God and those who looked to her for help. So the friend who wrote von Hügel for aid had, as most seekers have done, come a long way toward clarification before she ever sought his help and direction. Then as now, these hunches, these intimations, these preliminary clarifications may still be ever so evanescent, and ever so readily lost. What they need is the confirmation, establishment, and sinking of roots, the challenging and rephrasing in the face of the challenge which can so often be effected only by going over them again before God in the presence of another. Hence the call for help.

Von Hügel's reply to her had about it the feeling of the entire naturalness of one Christian coming to another in this way. He once told his niece, 'One torch lights another. . . . It is best to learn from others; it gives a touch of creatureliness,' and in his reply to Evelyn Underhill he does not seem surprised at all, but only expresses his deep thankfulness and confirmation of what is beginning to come clear to her.

> You evidently realized why and where I was hoping and praying for a development in you . . . what I directly and clearly wanted for you was just what you now tell me you have gained and won! Deo Gratias. I congratulate you and beg you to persevere most faithfully in all that is positive in this your new and, I pray, confirmed outlook. Of course you will have dryness, disgust, strong inclinations to revert to the more or less pure 'mysticism'. But it is excellent news that, preparing one of these addresses for Manchester College, Oxford, you found that you had really come out strongly and self-committingly for Traditional, Institutional, Sacramental Religion.[11]

The next letter which followed on this one, where he had confirmed her hunch that she must recover for her own religious life and interpretation the centrality of the institutional element, contains a strong word of caution about pressing this new insight too far, too fast. He notes the operation of a kind of

11 *Evelyn Underhill*, Margaret Cropper. New York: Harper, p. 69.

Boyle's law in the spiritual world that tends to make the intoxication with the most recent discovery result in an almost inevitably violent depreciation of all states that immediately preceded it, and writes, 'As a matter of fact I fear for you as much the over-doing of institutionalism as the ignoring or even flying from it: indeed these two extremes are twin sisters in such a soul as yours.'[12] He follows this by a minimal institutional program for her own personal nurture, yet one that he encourages her to stick to through times of consolation and desolation without much alteration: one church service on Sunday, preferably the early communion in her own Anglican church, and a mid-week visit to an early convent service in a house which is well known to her.

He trails this cautiously by a further reservation, 'Perhaps even these two practices are too much for the minimum, since, of course, not the resolution alone but the execution matters really, and I should wish to save you above all things, from any real overburdening.'[13] Here he is seen fitting his counsel to a high-strung person who while in less danger than most of substituting religiosity for religion, might very well be overburdened by the institutional and be driven into a subsequent revulsion for it. Then he lays down for private devotions, her 'deliberate praying', a maximum of half an hour a day for prayer together with a three to five minute examination of conscience at night before retiring. The prayerful disposition that penetrates all she does is the one unrationable blessing in which he encourages her.

Some Laboratory Proposals

One religious retreat a year seems in order to him and it may be of several days' duration, but he warns her against membership in any religious guild or order at this stage. He characteristically suggests the cultivation of some non-religious interest such as music, painting, or gardening. To all of this, he adds a major suggestion of two afternoons a week to be devoted to 'visiting the poor'. This final prescription he suggests will do more than anything that he can propose to thaw out the cerebral accent in her religion and to break open her heart to the needs of all. In the course of doing this, it may help her to realize increasingly how little her sophisticated religion is able to speak to the needs of these people.

12. *Evelyn Underhill*. Margaret Cropper. New York: Harper, p. 71.
13. *Ibid*. p. 71.

I believe you ought to get yourself, gently and gradually, interested in the poor; that you should visit them, very quietly and unostentatiously, with as little incorporation as possible into Visiting Societies, etc. You badly want de-intellectualizing or at least developing homely human sense and spirit dispositions and activities . . . it will, if properly entered into and persevered with, discipline, mortify, deepen and quiet you. It will, as it were, distribute your blood—some of your blood—away from your brain, where too much is lodged at present. And if and when religion does appear on the scene, you will find how homely, how much of sense as well as spirit it has and had to be. Again, how excellent for you! For what is a religion which cannot mean anything to the uneducated poor? . . . I would carefully give preference to the two weekly visitations of the poor above everything else, excepting definite home and family duties, or any express wishes of your husband—in each case as distinct from your own likes and dislikes.[14]

He does not cut her off entirely from her own work of spiritually counseling others, but suggests the wisdom of cutting it down for the immediate future and of avoiding taking on new cases.

On the matter of her very deep emotional involvement in her friendships with women, he suggests that these may be a compensation for the overintellectual character of her theocentric religion and that if this religion could broaden its base, some of this craving for these possessive friendships might abate. He counsels a gentle detachment within attachment, a holding of these persons up to God and keeping this Ground of friendship always to the fore.

More important than any of this, however, would seem to have been von Hügel's effort to get her to face the neglected share of the incarnational aspect in her religious life: of what Jesus Christ was and what he revealed about God, and to get this into the warp and woof of her thought and practice. He knew from her books that she was no theosophist, that in addition to the theocentric approach there was a deep respect for what Jesus Christ had brought into the world. But beyond a distant respect and admiration, he found none of it either in the frames of thought in which she was interpreting the Christian religion or in her personal life of prayer.

14. *Evelyn Underhill*, Margaret Cropper. New York: Harper, p. 75.

In seeing the director of souls at work at this point, there is first of all no forcing. With such a commanding mind as hers, it is clear to him that she must face the main issue and not by-pass it, if she is to move at all. It is only what she is convinced really *is*, and not what ought to be, that can ultimately hold her. He seeks first of all to get her consent to the proposition that at least some Historical Happenings are necessary to the Christian religion. He notes that she occasionally writes as if the Christian religion would be entirely unaffected if all these Historical Happenings were shown to be false. He asks for a decision on this ambiguity in her approach, and suggests that she consider whether the time has not come 'gradually but most thoroughly' to drop this non-historical attitude. This step taken, he asks if she is prepared to see in Jesus Christ, God revealing himself, and secondly if she is prepared to see in Jesus Christ such a difference of degree of self-revelation as to constitute a difference of kind? If she can go this far, she can postpone action on the virgin birth, the Johannine miracles, and the resurrection.

George Fox once said to a seeker, 'Look to that which is good in you to lead you to God'. With Evelyn Underhill von Hügel was also prepared to start where she was and to move on from there. 'Simply feed your soul on the great positive facts and truths you see already : pray for fidelity to your light, and for as much light as may be within God's plan for you. And as for the rest, neither force adhesion nor allow rejection, but let it alone, as possible food for others and indeed for yourself later on. It does not concern *yourself at present*.'[15]

As for her prayers, he proposed no sudden giving up of her natural theocentric approach. This approach is after all an indispensable movement in the life of prayer. The suggestion rather was to start by asking only for an abandonment of the notion of its exclusiveness and the entertaining at least of the possibility of its being crossed with the incarnational accent. Could she begin by admitting that the theocentric approach is not *the* way to pray but is rather *a* way to pray? Could she perhaps pray in her theocentric way to the unincarnate God and then bring into the foreground Nazareth and the Lake of Galilee and Calvary in order to see what 'the incarnation might have been like and what it cost to 'come all the way downstairs'? It is with this kind of gentleness that his guidance was given.

15. *Evelyn Underhill*, Margaret Cropper. New York: Harper, p. 96.

All Custom-Guidance is Subject to Drastic Modification

The agreement between them was that she was to report to him first of all, each six months, and then in 1923-24, once a year. Her reports are searching and bring his swift response. Once again, his guidance is individual and not by rule of thumb. She has been in a time of desolation! She must scale down drastically the supposed fixed minimum that was to be carefully preserved in consolation *and in desolation* and take up some manual work which in this case turned out to be a return to the Middle Ages by taking up script writing. She found the need for more than one retreat in a year at the Anglican retreat center of Pleshey. She must, of course, have two. Later she feels a need for a longer time of deliberate prayer each day. She must extend the time.

She has had recurrences of her terrible doubts that the whole religious life is only a human projection, is purely subjective. Here von Hügel is firm and sharp with her. 'You should see my old man dusting me down,' she once said to Lucy Menzies. Can she deny that universality of human need for facing the claim-fulness of the surface self on the one hand or the dealing with that need by God and Christ on the other? Do not these facts constitute a snubbing of the loose line that has let her skeptical fancies run free? Or again, she has miscast herself in the wrong ascetical type. She is no Trappist type, no de Rancé. Readiness to abandon her temperamental fancies and inclinations, her over-concern with herself and her failures, to take what God sends her, to carry on all that she does for God, this is the form of the ascetical call for her.

She feels her unreadiness for intercessory prayer and mentions her wincing before the possible price of such prayer. Graham Greene has recently said much of this price in his searching play *The Potting Shed* in connection with the priest uncle's inter-cessory prayer for his nephew's life. 'As to intercession,' wrote Evelyn Underhill to von Hügel, 'if I ask myself whether I could face complete spiritual deprivation for the good of another: e.g., to affect a conversion, I can't do that yet. So I have not got real Christian love: and the question is, can one intercede genuinely for anyone, unless he is ready to pay, if necessary, this price.'[16]

16. *Evelyn Underhill*, Margaret Cropper. New York: Harper, p. 107

Salesian Gentleness in Spiritual Guidance

Once again von Hügel shows a truly Salesian gentleness. She is not to strain after the practice of intercession for others. She is to be very faithful in visits to the poor and in taking the sacraments. She had better go on with her ordinary prayer and in time, perhaps soon, a call to intercession will come. Von Hügel wrote her, 'We must always in our own efforts strive to reach what we have not got by the faithful practice of what we have, although God is in no way tied in his dealings with us to this procedure.'[17]

Always he tried to draw her quietly away from that inverse form of pride that beats its breast at its own cowardly impotence, its spiritual misery, at its own weakness, and into a consciousness that with the focus on God and Christ and their redemptive action, the self is really transformed. 'Develop a general, gradually increasing habit of dropping all voluntary self-absorption during the day and gently turn to God in Christ . . . a gentle, general horror of self and a simple flight away from self to God and Christ—to Christ—God—this will brace you finely.' 'Drop gently, drop by a quiet burning to God and Christ and the poor, and you will grow in peace and power.'[18]

William Russell Maltby once counseled his fellow clergy about their sermons: 'One word on sin and nine on the Redeemer,' and von Hügel's spiritual counsel carried this same glint. Encourage by directing the mind of the one who prays upon the ultimate source of encouragement. The rest will take care of itself.

Through all of these four years of guidance, there is one further facet that dare not be neglected. For von Hügel, from beginning to end, Evelyn Underhill was a special child of God. She had a special vocation to fulfil. She had a genius that if put to apostolic use might greatly further the kingdom. While he encouraged her to write less, 'say two-thirds of your output during the average of the last ten years', and to cut down for a time on her own guidance of souls, it is all with the utter confidence that God will in his good time release her again for her vocation freshly endued with power from on high. Her call to sanctity, to be possessed by the One for whom she was made, must come within

17. *Evelyn Underhill*, Margaret Cropper, New York: Harper, p. 95.
18. *Ibid.* pp. 111 and 124.

the strength and limitation of her body, her mind, her nervous system, her station in life, and this sanctity will come if she will yield to it.

Out of these years of direction that closed only with von Hügel's death in 1925, there emerged a new orientation in Evelyn Underhill's life and writing. As with so many of his friends, she did not become a Roman Catholic but was drawn more deeply than ever before into the life of her own Anglican communion. She wrote to Dom John Chapman, 'I owe him (v. H.) my whole spiritual life, and there would have been more of it than there is, if I had been more courageous and stern with myself, and followed his directions more thoroughly.'[19]

> Until about five years ago I never had *any* personal experience of our Lord. I didn't know what it meant. . . . Somehow by his (v. H's) prayers or something, he compelled me to experience Christ. He never said anything more about it—but I knew humanly speaking he did it. It took about four months—it was like watching the sun rise very slowly—and then suddenly one knew what it was.
>
> Now for some months after that I remained predominantly theocentric. But for the next two or three years and especially lately, more and more my whole religious life and experience seemed to center with increasing vividness in our Lord—that sort of quasi-involuntary prayer which springs up of itself at odd moments is always now directed to Him.[20]

From this time, her own guidance of souls, her increasing service as a retreat leader at Pleshey into which she poured her best thinking and insights during the last fifteen years of her life, and her books and letters take on a new tone and focus. What she learned for herself from von Hügel's direction, she gave costingly and with a moving abandon to others.

This case study of von Hügel's guidance of Evelyn Underhill does not in any way exhaust the materials at our disposal in studying the Baron's gift in spiritual counsel. The volume of *Letters to a Niece* is still in print and this in itself contains a most revealing look into his handling of a young woman on the threshold of life. The correspondence with both George Tyrrell and Maude Petre is also full of this kind of guidance, as are occasional letters to people in every station of life, to say nothing

19. *Evelyn Underhill*, Margaret Cropper. New York: Harper, p. 68.
20. *Ibid.* p. 98.

of the rich sprinkling of counsel that is interlarded throughout his philosophical and theological books.

The Pharmaceutical Chest of Spiritual Guidance

What is there to be said in general about the prescriptions of spiritual guidance? What are they meant to do? In one of the Gospel stories, a group of men powerless of themselves to heal a paralytic, were able nevertheless to bear him to the house where Jesus was teaching and to elude the crowd by lowering him from the roof into the presence of the one who was alone able to heal him. All spiritual guidance and devotional practice has for its function only this business of eluding the crowd, of carrying, of bearing, of bringing the persons to be guided more directly into the Healing Presence and then to leave them there. God Himself is the real spiritual director.

There is, however, almost never anything new in this pharmaceutical chest of spiritual guidance. There are no 'wonder drugs', no revolutionary surgical instruments, no radioactive applications. Yet the old tested medicines are forever being adapted by a good physician to the special needs of the patient and we can most profitably examine von Hügel as he goes about this work of adaptation.

Of all of these remedies directed at a cure for the inevitable dispersions of life in this world, none is more universally applicable than prayer. 'The Christian spirit is a matter of daily self-conquest,' von Hügel wrote to Wilfred Ward in 1875, and in that daily matter, von Hügel confessed that he could not get on without the regular use of prayer. Some of this prayer would no doubt be vocal and often in the form of the great classic prayers of mankind. To know that one is not praying alone but is lifted up into a great common tide of prayer is usually a substantial help and very especially in the midst of suffering when single phrases or even words repeated over and over are hand-holds that one requires. If these bear us into the Presence, that is all that is necessary. But beyond this (although not necessarily above it) is mental prayer and after its obvious phases of repentance and forgiveness, there usually emerges a season of intercession.

Von Hügel says little of the form that his own intercessions took, but he once wrote to his niece,

I wonder whether you realize a deep, great fact? That souls—all human souls—are deeply interconnected. That we can not only pray for each other, but *suffer* for each other? That these long, trying wakings [his 'white nights'], that I was able to offer them to God and to Christ for my child—that He might ever strengthen, sweeten, steady her in her true, simple, humble love and dependence upon Him? Nothing is more real than this interconnection—this gracious power put by God into the very heart of our infirmities.[21]

Here is the kernel of Charles Williams' insight into what it means to carry one another, the theme about which his novel *Descent into Hell* is written. And here is the reason why intercession may end with no more than Catherine of Genoa's 'for these I cannot ask anything from this tender Love: I can but present them in His presence.'[22] Yet in other cases, that carrying may bring the bearer as low as St. Christopher's divine burden brought him at mid-stream. Von Hügel clearly had both kinds in mind and the number of friends that he carried in intercession morning, noon, and night was never small.

For von Hügel, the highest dimension in prayer was that of adoration. For here there is no self-concern, no 'flea hunting' for sins, no business to transact; only an overwhelming thankfulness that God is what he is and has done what he has done, only the fulfilled 'longing aye to dwell within the beauty of His countenance', to know that 'we are not He—but He made us', to know that the abyss of his mysterious love is never plumbed, and yet that he gives himself to us forever. It is to be noted that on von Hügel's tombstone in Stratton-on-the-Fosse there is chiseled the psalmist's cry of adoration, 'Whom have I in heaven but Thee?'

For those for whom the movements of repentance, forgiveness, intercession and adoration give way to the involuntary prayer of simple regard, von Hügel has only encouragement. But he gives many hints that the ordinary movements of 'deliberate prayer' are still a part of his daily ration. He also suggests that to remember God as we move from one occupation to another throughout the day is good, and that it helps to cultivate that quiet sense of his presence back of all that we do.

Remedial Instruction in Devotional Reading

Again and again in his letters there are references to his daily fifteen minutes which he gave to devotional reading. 'And I have

21. *Selected Letters*, London: Dent, 1927, p. 269.
22. *The Mystical Element of Religion*. London: Dent, 1908, Vol. II, p. 127.

been so hard worked that, for this kind of reading, I can only find my usual quarter of an hour; which has to go to those few books (*Bible* and *Imitation* and *Confessions*) which have been my staple food hitherto,'[23] or once more, 'that daily quarter of an hour for now forty years or more, I am sure has been one of the great sustenances and sources of calm for my life.'[24] St. Augustine : I cannot exaggerate the gain that I think you will derive from feeding for years on the *Confession*. They, more than any other book, excepting the Gospels and the Psalms, have taught me and I believe they will teach you.'[25] 'I am so glad you are trying to work the *Imitation* (*of Christ*) into your life : it is the only way to read it which is really worthy of what itself is so intensely alive. Now *there* is a book written as should be all religious books; they should be the quintessence of a long experience and fight in suffering and self-transformation.'[26]

This devotional reading, von Hügel believed, is to be done to lift the sights. It is to re-engage the soul in its divine vocation. It is read in the hope that some phrase or line in it may single out the reader's condition, may be an occasion on which God may speak to him, may perhaps convict him of sin or of untilled ground in his life that he has been reserving, or may lure him on in something that may have long since been undertaken but which is lagging.

This kind of reading is there to be distinguished from ordinary reading and his words to his niece about the way to read a devotional book show the seasoned spiritual guide at work once again. Here is a whole set of lessons in remedial reading packed into a single letter.

Of course such '*reading*' *is hardly reading in the ordinary sense at all*. As well could you call the letting a very slowly dissolving lozenge melt imperceptibly in your mouth, eating. Such reading is, of course, meant as directly as possible to feed the heart, to fortify the will,—to put these into contact with God—thus, by the book, to get away from the book, to the realities it suggests. . . . And, above all, perhaps it excludes, by its very object, all criticism, all going off on one's own thoughts as in any way antagonistic to the book's thoughts; and this not by any unreal (and most dangerous) forcing of oneself to

23. *Selected Letters*. London : Dent, 1927, p. 203.
24. *Ibid.* p. 229.
25 *Ibid.* p. 279.
26. *Ibid.* p. 229.

swallow, or to 'like' what does not attract one's simply humble self, but (on the contrary) by a gentle passing by, by an instinctive ignoring of what does not suit one's soul. This passing by should be without a trace of would-be objective judging; during such reading, we are out simply and solely to feed our own poor soul, such as it is here and now. What repels or confuses us now, may be the food of angels; it may even still become the light to our own poor soul's dimness. We must exclude none of such possibilities, 'the infant crying for the light' has nothing to do with more than just humbly finding, and then using the little light that *it* requires.

I need not say that I would not restrict you to only one quarter of an hour a day. You might find two such helpful. But I would not exceed fifteen minutes *at any one time*; you would sink to ordinary reading if you did.[27]

This most generous of men was always buying and sending off packets of books to his friends and correspondents, and apart from the basic fare already mentioned, the writings of two eighteenth-century French devotional authors were much in favor. Père Caussade's *Self-Abandonment to Divine Providence* and Père Grou's *Manual of Inner Souls*.

There was always a clear distinction between this special devotional reading to be done in its own way, almost in the mood of meditation, and the wide ranging voracious ordinary reading in history, biography, literature, philosophy and science that he was constantly about himself and that in due moderation he commended to others. He was horrified at the rumors that the high Anglican, Pusey, read only religious books. For himself, von Hügel had a bee's lack of fastidiousness in his willingness to gather honey from any available flower. But with all this, specifically devotional reading found its unique and indispensable place in the day's menu.

The Tarnished Mounting and the Jewel

His third prescription to those he guided was that they participate actively in corporate worship. His writings are crammed with ardent testimony to the importance he attached to the corporate aspect of religion. While von Hügel has been popularly known for his championing of the mystical element in religion,

27. *Selected Letters*. London: Dent, 1927, p. 229.

a more careful scrutiny of his writings might seriously qualify
this impression, and might compel an acknowledgment that his
peculiar contribution had tended rather to emphasize the very
special necessity of crossing the mystical with the historical and
institutional. 'Thus mysticism would never be the whole of religion : it would become a dangerous error the very moment it
claimed to be the whole; but at the same time it would be an
element essential to religion in the long run and upon the whole,
although it would, as already said, possess its own dangers, its
own besetting sins.'[28]

Repeatedly he points out the vocational excesses and ex-
travagances of the mystic, the mystic's bent to individualism, to
pantheism, and the rest. Von Hügel's goal seems always to be
that of bringing the mystical element back into a creative tension
with the historical and institutional, to finding the nail-marked
foot of Jesus Christ planted squarely in the door of any such
excess and demanding a reckoning, on the part of the mystic,
with the historical Jesus and with the institutional conduit of his
message to them, namely the Christian Church.

Here in this historical figure of Jesus Christ with which the
corporate worship of the Church confronts us, we are back in
the company of something greater than ourselves, yet something
that as the new Adam, the type man, as the revelation of God,
and as the focus of redemptive love, searches and probes our
every need and aspiration. Nor is this any local phenomena. Von
Hügel in a famous passage insists that in this corporate confrontation, we meet One whom all the ages and races and civil-
izations will never exhaust,

> For a person came and lived and loved, and did and taught,
> and died and rose again, and lives on by His Spirit forever
> within us and amongst us, so unspeakably rich and yet so
> simple, so sublime and yet so homely, so divinely above us
> precisely in being so divinely near,—that His character and
> teaching require for an ever fuller yet never complete under-
> standing, the varying study, and different experiments and
> applications, embodiments and unrollings of all the races and
> civilizations, of all the individual and corporate, the simul-
> taneous and successive experiences of the human race to the
> end of time.[29]

28. *The Reality of God.* London: Dent, 1931, p. 91.
29. *The Mystical Element of Religion.* London: Dent. 1908, Vol. I, p. 26.

The Church, for all of its shortcomings, its failures, its blasphemies, its apostasy (and von Hügel although a Roman Catholic, is the last either to deny or even to conceal them), this hair shirt of some form of institutional religion and of its regular exercises of corporate worship cannot be by-passed but must become a part of the practice of a sin-ridden, short-memoried, flesh-and-blood pilgrim who would let God have His way with him in this life. For von Hügel, the Church, 'at its best and deepest, is just that—that interdependence of all the broken and the meek, all the self-oblivion, all the reaching out to God and souls',[30] and if the skeletal structure of different ecclesiastical organizations offends the angel-like vision of many, including his niece, as to what the ideal Church should be like, the old baron reminds her in his quaint way that 'even Cleopatra, when in the splendor of her youth, had such a very useful, very necessary, quite unavoidable skeleton inside her, had she not?'[31]

Deep as is his respect for the spiritual and social witness of the Quakers, von Hügel is never tired of reminding them that they lack a deep enough sense of gratitude for the Bible, for the saints, and for the preservation of the active and regular confrontation by the historical Christ which has come down through history in the Church. For him, this regular confrontation of the worshiper by the historic Christ is an essential, and the Church is the tarnished mounting in which the jewel of Christ is set.

His own view of the Church was naturally closely bound up with sacramental practice. There is something moving in the reports of scholarly companions who occasionally accompanied him on his daily walk on Hampstead Heath. One has spoken of how they were passing the little Catholic chapel on the Heath just as he was making some devastatingly critical remarks on a New Testament text, and of how he hastily excused himself, entered the chapel, sank down on his knees before the sacrament on the altar, and lost himself in prayer. For him there was apparently no incongruity between the free mind and scrupulous adherence to devotional practice. One of his happiest remarks referred to those who were very firm at the center, being able to be quite free at the periphery.

No one in his generation felt more deeply the neglect of the intellectual and scientific element in religion on the part of the Roman Catholic Church or wrote more openly to his friends

30. *Selected Letters*. London: Dent, 1927, pp. 269–270.
31. *Ibid.* p. 270.

about the heavy-handed authoritarian pressures that were used to stamp out the modernistic movement in which he played a prominent role. In fact, in 1910, he wrote to Maude Petre of his anticipation of his own excommunication and asked her prayers 'and please pray for me that, if and when my trial comes, I may be most carefully, most faithful to my best lights as God may give them to me.'[32] Why it did not come has been so frequently discussed as to preclude repetition, but while such an experience unquestionably exercised a restraining hand on any zeal he might have had for encouraging non-Catholics to enter the Roman Catholic Church, it did not modify in the least his profound emphasis upon the necessity of corporate worship and of some historic institutional connection in the nurture and growth of a soul in the Christian faith.

He had himself lived deeply in fifteenth century, pre-Council of Trent, Renaissance Catholicism. It was from that age that he had chosen the married laywoman mystic, Catherine of Genoa, to form the focus of his study in the *Mystical Element*. He tells us, too, that he longs to write on Nicholas of Cusa, the great fifteenth-century Catholic philosopher, mystic, and humanist. Perhaps all of this helped develop in him an acute understanding and appreciation of the elements of truth contained in other religious institutions than his own. Yet whether he is speaking to the Anglicans, Evelyn Underhill and Dean Inge, or to the Quaker, Rufus Jones, all three of whom acknowledged their enormous spiritual debt to him, he insisted that no soul is saved alone, and that the personal neglect of the corporate worship of God can only lead to a tragic impoverishment. Such worship can and has helped to rid the soul of an over-isolated individualism and fastidiousness, has helped to elicit from it a great wholesome sense of creatureliness, and has served to bind it to Jesus Christ as a member of a costly redemptive community that dissolves away all barriers.

Corporate Worship and the Achilles' Heel of Psychotherapy

Less to the fore, but no less real, in von Hügel's guidance of souls is the fact that the Church and the practice of corporate worship provides something that keeps the counseling relationship clean. A generation later, the contrast between the inclusion of corporate worship and the situation in ordinary secularized

32. *Selected Letters.* London: Dent, 1927, p. 185.

psychotherapy is very striking. For in the close and inevitably dependent relation in which a person stands to the other person guiding him or acting as his therapeutic counselor, certain highly destructive adhesions almost inevitably appear. The significance of these 'transference' phenomena has still to be plumbed to its root by psychotherapy, but many therapists find they are so cumbersome and leave such lasting scars, that they have tried all manner of strategems including even the mixing in of group therapy with individual therapy in order to try to rid themselves of his highly vulnerable Achilles' heel or at least to attempt to moderate its effects.

When the one who guides and the one who is guided both re-quire and are regularly engaged in corporate worship, they are swept out of themselves, out of their superior and dependent roles, out of their self-occupation in which all therapy and guid-ance abounds, and into the presence of One who fulfills and satisfies and not only discloses their need but who renews their courage to live toward him. Here is an objective cleansing that places the whole relationship on a new basis.

At its best there is in all corporate worship an objective, unself conscious therapy going on that lays hold of any self-conscious therapy that has preceded it, and consummates it. Yet without this act of corporate worship, which always follows the therapeutic processes when these are a part of the normal apparatus of the Christian Church, there is prolonged self-absorption and a network of dependency relationships in therapy that even the most brilliant contributions in the field in recent years have not been able fully to untangle. The regular return to the objectivity of worship, to the confrontation with Jesus Christ, to the self-losing belonging to a redemptive community on the part of both guide and guided, furnished a setting for the thera-peutic situation that von Hügel felt to be essential.

On Lightening Ship in Times of Dryness

Evelyn Underhill promptly turned von Hügel's spiritual counsel into a rule of life for herself, and it is true that the prac-tice of preparing such a simple rule of life, of submitting it to the spiritual director, and, after securing his approval, of living by it and then, after a time, revising it in order to make it a more suitable regimen, is a customary formula in spiritual guid-ance. But von Hügel knew in advance that rough times would come and that even the commitment to a simple rule would tend to be shaken by these inevitable spells of spiritual dryness, these times of inward consolidation, of testing, of what Evelyn Underhill tellingly calls being put on 'the night shift'. Well in advance, he warns those he guides about these times, and tells them if necessary to lighten ship on their rules until the rough time is over.

> Now what I advise you to do, when spiritual dryness comes markedly into your soul, is to drop all your continuous though mixed prayer—all, that is, except short morning and night prayer; little aspirations during the day, especially acceptances of this dryness; and on Sundays, your Holy Communion . . . ; as soon as without self-probing you see that the dry bout is over, quietly resume your full rule—not till then. . . . Treat your soul as the captains in the old pre-steam days treated their crew. These men had always to be busy, but not always sailing. Weeks of no wind, or of the wrong wind would keep them from sailing. What then! They would at once, as part of their work and life, drop the sailing and take to the mending and making of sails and nets, etc. So do you.[33]

Rules are made for men, not men for rules, and once again the great sanity of von Hügel shines through.

Religious Practice and the Broad Overlap with Common Life

Von Hügel looked upon retreats, that is withdrawing to an appointed house for several days of silence, prayer and religious instruction, as a helpful auspice if they were well conducted and not attended at too frequent intervals. Above all, he does not wish to overtax those he guides, and he fears religiosity like the plague. There were several devices to this end of cauterizing religiosity which he used himself and which he commended to others in the solid guidance that he gave them. He believed that a fairly broad overlap with people in all walks of life helped greatly. He found in the duties and celebrations of his own family an immeasurable boon. He found that his walks in the public gardens daily which brought him close to children and nursemaids were good for him and much prized in his life.

33. *Evelyn Underhill.* Margaret Cropper, New York: Harper, 1958, p. 97.

Once more, my Swedish friend Emelia Fogelklou-Norlind has written me of her visit to von Hügel and his family in 1921, eleven years after her first London visit in 1910, when he stood under the pall of impending religious troubles.

Tall, upright, without any resting-chair, stately with radiant and clear eyes under shaggy brows, he came to meet me looking at least ten years younger than last time. (I should have liked to see him in Kensington Gardens just beyond with his little Pekinese dog, and a lot of children who without hesitation chose *him* to tell them the time of day by his watch.) Instead I saw him this time as a pater familiae. The merry family lunch at the big round table was unlike the twilight hours in 1910. . . . He was so full of hope, so happy, and also so full of jokes. And when he gave his last greeting at my taking leave, he did not now speak of the duty to suffer and to bear the pain of it, but of the wonderful *Joy to live*! In the copy of Julian of Norwich's *Revelations* which he gave me as a present, he wrote in his big square handwriting, 'This shewed our good Lord, to make us glad and merry'.

In addition to these ordinary duties heartily performed, von Hügel had a prescription which he had tried on himself and found most bracing. As has been mentioned, he conceived of science and its rigorous discipline of objectivity as a kind of asceticism especially suited to our age and he counseled anyone who spent much time in religious affairs to master the discipline of at least one science thoroughly. He had been a lifelong student of geology and later had been much involved in textual criticism, and he felt that both of these sciences checked his trying to see things according to his subjective preference and were just the friction that was needed by one in whom the inner life was a primary concern. Furthermore this hard, cold, scientific discipline strengthened the intellectual element and its integrity as one of the elements of the religious life itself.

Heroic Goodness and the Supernatural

Von Hügel's spiritual direction quite naturally aimed at kindling such a fierce love of God that only a life of sanctity would suffice. And sanctity means not only a growing yielding to God but it means suffering and joy, and it means heroic virtue in this

world. All around him he found flashes of the supernatural, of
another order breaking through into this order in the acts of heroic
virtue that tumbled out of ordinary people: a busman, an Irish
washerwoman, a territorial soldier, all appeared in face of the
wholly unpredictable, uncontrollable, unevadable events that life
poured out upon them. For von Hügel, these acts are different
from the natural, 'Thus bodily cleanliness, honesty in buying
and selling, submission to the police and due tax-paying to the
state . . . all was indeed held to be from God, to be necessary, to
be good. But it was only Natural Good.' Von Hügel is not against
this substratum. But for a Christian, it is not enough. Someone
has suggested that if you want to be good, you have got to be
heroically good, and von Hügel is pointing to something of the
same temper. 'A religion is not worth much if it does not produce
heroic acts,' von Hügel suggests.

> God . . . has put salt in our mouths, and we now thirst for
> what we have experienced. We now long for Supernatural
> Good. Supernatural Beatitude. Now acts, acts and dispositions
> become possible, attractive, even actual within us and by us,
> which no State, no Guild can ever presuppose or require. Now
> decency is carried up into devotedness and homeliness and
> heroism. This is the real and unique work of the Church! 'the
> awakening, the training, the bringing into full life and fruitful-
> ness of the supernatural life.'[34]

And this too is the goal of all genuine spiritual direction.

But *'awakening, training, bringing into full life and fruitfulness of the supernatural life,'* clearly this is nothing that a
spiritual director can accomplish! This is a task for the Grace of
God. For who would dare to claim that he had a formula of basic
training for the eruption into being of such heroic life? Or who
would dare lay down any rules for what by its very nature is
beyond rules, for what astonishes, for what makes us all bow
before its authenticity, and yet which must come up from the
deep upon an occasion that is anything but deliberate?

Yet even here, von Hügel suggests that some hints are not out
of place. One of the universal occasions where this heroism may
appear is in the midst of physical and mental suffering in which
all men at some time share. Von Hügel gives no suggestion that

34. *Essays and Addresses on the Philosophy of Religion.* London: Dent,
1921, 1st series, p. 283.

Christianity has an explanation of suffering. It acknowledges it for the evil thing it is. But while it has no explanation, Jesus Christ, the One who has gone before, has shown the way to transform it and it is this transformation of the unpredictable extremity into an instrument in the service of God which is the indelible mark of heroic virtue, of the emergence of the supernatural.

Holy Suffering is the Crown of Holy Action

How, then, may a Christian deal with suffering? He, too, may with God's help transform it and make it the thin place in the membrane where the supernatural shows through. One of the things about suffering which von Hügel notes as especially favourable for taking us beyond those things we can manage in our own strength, is that in it we cannot pretend and put on airs. 'We cannot, do what we will, cut a decent figure in our own eyes.' Rather we are ruthlessly cut down to size. It is in the midst of pain that we have a chance to learn to whom we belong, on whom we can depend, or on whom we may rest our trust when we may be too weak even to lay it there. Here, von Hügel, in some of the most noble teaching to be found in Christian literature on the bearing of pain, teaches us how, when we cannot bear to face it in blocks of a month or a week or a day or an hour, we can face it in terms of this single pain, and the offering up to God of this pain 'with the pain well mixed up into the prayer' as a redemptive gift or as an act of intercession for sin, 'O may this pang deepen me, may it help to make me real, real— really humble, really loving, really ready to live or die with my soul in Thy hands.' 'Oh! Oh! This is real : oh! deign to accept it, as a little real atonement for real sin.'[35] In 1921 he wrote to his niece of these unexpected occasions of suffering when God gives us concomitant opportunities and graces and growths, 'Holy suffering is the very crown of holy action. And God is no pedant. He can and does look to the substance of our suffering and knows how to penetrate beyond our surface restlessness.'[36]

He believed that any occasion could be the occasion of the supernatural disclosing itself, and he had a great passion for selecting simple occasions like the very unpleasant one of packing, which his niece resisted, and showing her how this business might be one that could be lifted to God and made the occasion of serving

35. *Selected Letters*. London : Dent, 1927, p. 231.
36. *Ibid.* p. 390.

him with joy and gladness. In fact, as von Hügel continues in his guidance, there is almost nothing of the stuff of ordinary life that could not become such an occasion of concomitant Grace, given our deep enough yielding. This is where he brings in his dependence upon the saints for teaching us here on earth that God's joy can be found anywhere, and he notes how the saints serve us by making 'goodness attractive' and making the plainest acts sing like Paul and Silas in their prison cell. Again and again, von Hügel notes that in the canonization of the saint by the Roman Catholic Church, not only heroic virtue, but joy, abandoned, reckless, uncalculating joy, must shine through and be present as an indispensable condition of meeting the requirements.

He sought to live as he taught, and at the close of his life, when he knew he was dying and that he would never be able to finish the Gifford Lectures which he had been dictating and working on up to these days, he said gaily, 'I wait for the breath of God, for God's breath. Perhaps he will call me today—tonight. Don't let us be niggardly towards God. He is never a niggard towards us.—Let us try to be generous and accept. . . . I would like to finish my book—but if not, I shall live it out in the Beyond.'[37]

His final words to his niece whose young life he had sought to awaken to the call of God beyond the ordinary line of duty, are words that seem fitting to close a treatment of his role as a spiritual director:

Our great hope is in Christianity—our only hope. Christ re-creates. Christianity has taught us to care. Caring is the greatest thing—caring matters most. My faith is not enough—it comes and goes. I have it about some things and not about others. So we make up and supplement each other. We give and others give to us. Keep your life, a life of prayer, dearie. . . . Keep it like that: it's the only thing, and remember, no joy without suffering—no patience without trial—no humility without humiliation—no life without death.[38]

37. *Letters to a Niece*, Gwendolyn Greene. London: Dent, 1928, p. xlii.
38. *Ibid.* p. xliii.

PART ONE

A SELECTION OF BARON FRIEDRICH
VON HÜGEL'S SPIRITUAL LETTERS

Chapter I

SPIRITUAL LETTERS: 1897-1909

T HE letters that follow in this chapter, while they were written
to a variety of persons, cover the period of von Hügel's intimate friendship with George Tyrrell. They are given in
chronological order and a brief commentary has been supplied in
introducing many of them.

The first letter is addressed to von Hügel's new-found friend,
George Tyrrell, whose spiritual gifts have already been revealed in a
series of moving books that have appeared. This letter does not give
but asks for spiritual help from Tyrrell for von Hügel's beloved elder
daughter, Gertrud, who has come into deep spiritual difficulties
which require other than a father's hand to unravel.

To George Tyrrell   (*October 19, 1897*)

I should particularly like to see you, for a reason which had
not loomed upon my horizon when I saw you ten days ago. My
dear close fellow-worker, my eldest daughter, is ordered by the
Doctor, as the only sure and swift cure for her sadly over-
wrought state of nerves and imagination, to get a six months'
complete change of environment. She will, therefore not accompany us abroad; and I see she much fancies, what I too would
much like, that she should come to you, if not for ordinary confession, at least occasionally for sympathy or advice. I have
watched and studied her ever since she was born, and her case
is in some respects peculiar. I should then be grateful if I could
have a good talk with you about her, and tho' I shall make a
point of coming down to you, if you cannot manage to come up
here, yet your coming would be in so far better, as it would prevent her thinking I was talking her over, which, in her present
somewhat abnormal state of health, she might mind. Before there
was any question of her seeing you, I told her I was hoping for a

second visit from you, so that your coming up would not give rise to any such surmises. . .

If you can come on Saturday, I shall also be able to introduce you to Mr. W. J. Williams, so shy and sensitive, thoughtful and original, and one of the five Catholic members of the 'Synthetic Society'. You would do him good.

Yours, dear Father Tyrrell,
With warm sympathy and gratitude,

VHT, pp. 14–15   F. von Hügel.

George Tyrrell had more than one visit with von Hügel's eldest daughter, Gertrud, and he wrote to the Baron that he had over-burdened the girl and that, 'if you want your daughter's company you must shorten your steps and walk slowly, else she will lose her breath in her desire to keep up with you.' He goes on to suggest that often we miss the way with those we counsel and that then, 'God has often to undo all our work for Him, and build it up again in his own way.' Von Hügel's reply reveals some of the personal agony out of which his own later gifts as a counselor have been forged.

To George Tyrrell   (Rome: January 26, 1898)

I know you will not have interpreted my renewed silence as in any way a want of agreement with, or of gratitude for, your second letter, as wise and helpful as both its predecessors. But, besides having much to do, and still but little health or heart to do it with, I wanted to get, if possible, some fresh facts or ideas to put to you, in this matter, which you will readily understand is constantly at least at the back of my mind, and which grows, in some ways, worse, not, please God, in itself, but in my mind. I see so increasingly plainly the triple fault and undermining character of my influence, the dwelling so constantly and freely on the detailed humanities in the Church; the drawing out and giving full edge to religious difficulties; the making too much of little intellectual and temperamental differences between myself and most Catholics, near relations included, so as to seriously weaken such influence as they might otherwise have had—Not but that all this was certainly unintended, unforseen : the grief and lasting keenness of the pain is, thank God, a sufficient proof of that : but, if only I had looked out against the selfishness of leaning on one whom I ought to have propped still for many a day ! I have dropped my own child, my first-born, whom God gave me to carry and to guard. I venture to come out with a little of what I am feeling in the matter, if only for this reason, that, whilst I do not feel it would be wise directly to say much more to G. about my grief and self-reproach, yet, it may be well that you should clearly know my frame of mind in the matter, as she might possibly take my, thank God, quite unforced, gentleness with her, and entirely undiminished love for her, as somehow indicating no very deep distress at her loss of light. I have for years felt in general and in several particular cases, and now feel more than ever in this case, how entirely a sense of *culpability* and a sense of loss, misfortune and danger are distinct: I feel no inclinations to the first, yet the entire absence of the first leaves quite undimmed and unblunted the keen consciousness of the second. What I think gives this keen edge to my feeling, is the anxiety and sort of dull dim consciousness that, for the moment, she has lost, not simply faith in the Church, and even the fundamental Christian dogma, but (which is surely a further and a still graver matter) true creatureliness of mind. And yet, as soon as I put this to myself, I have a joyful uncertainty after all, as to whether her mind has *set* on this point. I wrote her two days ago, and told her how this moral, humble, creaturely attitude towards God, one's own ideals, one's own achievements—the consciousness of incompleteness and of failure, of one's life being unlivable without its being lived cooperatively between the soul and God—how I found this in several friends who are no Catholics, no historic Christians of any kind; and that, as long as she can keep, and by daily practice and prayer ever regain this spirit, I can wait so far happily, quite indefinitely, as I should feel that she keeps in her the germ of full life, and is still living, in her degree, the one true life, and is still moving in the one true direction. I am clear that what I have said to her is very true and most consoling; there is, for instance, my good friend Professor Eucken of Jena (how I wish you read German, so as to read him)—how deeply creaturely his tone is; in moral disposition and view of life he is a Christian, though clearly stating and illustrating his non-acceptance of all dogma. I find it very hard to believe that even now, I mean before any reaction can be looked for, she has lost all such creatureliness, though imitation, and what not, may for the moment obscure it. I know that Abbé Huvelin (I have written to him now, but have not yet heard) used to say that many might think G.'s troubles came from simple pride; but that he found her very simple and often sweetly humble. If God preserves her that, even though hidden to herself and others, her face is turned in the right direction. I take it though that the spirit I mean cannot but suffer, for a while at least, under such a change, even though such a change need not have been preceded by the complete loss of that spirit; for I note with sadness that she seems turned, for the moment, away from moralism and spirituality, however general, however vague, to intellectualism, or even simple aestheticism. But that does not accord with her apparently unweakened simplicity; love of her little sister; attraction, still apparently, for such a tone as Père Grou's. Indeed, I am much struck at how quite recently still she was consulting me as to how and what books of his to get friends to read and work into their lives: this love of this childlike, creaturely spirit of Grou's which I feel to be the *fine fleur* of Christianity and of the Church...

VHT, pp. 20–24

Mrs Drew was the daughter of W. E. Gladstone in whose Cabinet von Hügel's father-in-law had once served. Von Hügel is writing to her upon the occasion of her father's death after a long illness. The reference to the role of suffering in the religious life and of heroic suffering as the highest and purest form of human action is a central note of his spiritual teaching and will recur again and again in his counsels.

To Mrs Henry Drew   (*4 Holford Road: May 23, 1898*)
Dear Mrs. Drew,

Mary wrote her letter of condolence to you on Saturday, without my knowing that this was so: I had wanted so much to add a line of my own, and I now venture to add one more note to the many, the endless number, that will be reaching you still.

It would indeed be conceit and pretentiousness, were I to attempt to praise or to discriminate. But I should much like to say one little word, though thousands have felt and said it already, each in their own way. Still, it is most entirely sincere, and hence may have its little place and little fruitfulness. It is this: that there is surely, for us Christians, no surer test of Faith on our part, nor truer proof of Love on God's part, than suffering nobly borne, and fully sent, and nothing that unites and reunites at all as does such suffering. And, if we all, and I with all, believed most truly in your ever admirably active earnest Father's goodness, even at a time when he could but show it by his actions, and when, from the very nature of the case, one could not always subscribe to more than his intentions: it was and is a consolation for us all, and for myself with all,—a pathetic and costing consolation—to have, during these months of most touching heroism, been most respectfully and completely at one with you his near and dear ones, in gratitude to God for the example and inspiration He has deigned to give us in your Father. I have always loved to think of devoted suffering as the highest, purest, perhaps the only quite pure form of action: and so it was a special grace and specially appropriate, that one as devoted and as active as your Father, should have been allowed and strengthened to practise the most devoted action possible for a sentient and rational creature of God.

I am, dear Mrs. Drew, with deep sympathy with you all,

> Yours sincerely,
>
> Fr. von Hügel.

SL, p. 70

There has been a good deal of discussion about precisely when von Hügel's sharp accent upon the given world of external things which science studies and which religion contemplates really made its first decisive appearance. Was it an insertion that came after the Roman Catholic church had so severely censured the subjectivist tendencies of the modernist movement from 1907 on, or was it integral to von Hügel's thought all along? This letter written to George Tyrrell before the end of the nineteenth century discloses the strong realist note to his thought and gives a clue to why as a spiritual counselor he demands that men respect the disciplined scientific study of the semi-autonomous world of nature and find in it an asceticism that can be most profitably used to balance out their natural inclination to a somewhat oversubjective, overemotional relationship with God. It also contains hints of his famous interpretation of sound religion as always a creative tension between the mystical-emotional, the scientific-intellectual, and the historical-institutional elements in its nature.

To George Tyrrell   (*4 Holford Road: September 26, 1898*)

I would like the teaching to run thus:

(*a*) As the body can live only by inhalation and exhalation, nutrition and evacuation, etc; and as the mind can only flourish by looking out for sensible material and then elaborating and spiritualising it: so the soul can live, to be fully normal in normal circumstances, only by a double process: occupation with the concrete and then abstraction from it, and this alternately, on and on. If it has not the latter it will grow empty and hazy, if it has not the former, it will grow earthly and heavy.

(b) Humanity at large is under *the strict obligation* (this, not simply because of the necessities of life, but *because of its spiritual perfection*) to practise *both these activities*: but at different periods excesses among the many, of one or other of these activities, justify and require counterbalancing, rectifying excesses of the opposite kind. And as the many will necessarily only exceed in the concrete direction, the compensating activity of the few will be in the abstracting direction. Still, the most difficult and yet most complete and most fruitful condition, and therefore the ideal, would be the plunging into the concrete and coming back enriched to the abstract, and then returning, purified and simplified, from the abstract to transform and elevate the concrete.

(c) The occupation with the concrete (I am primarily thinking of experimental science, critical scholarship, etc.) has profoundly changed or deepened its character, in proportion as the idea of *law*, of certain conditions, inexorably inherent to each observing mind, and to all observed matter, has become the necessary key to all work. Nature, history, all subjects of research first of all, now, present us with laws, with things, as neither the clamours of the petty self in front of them, nor, at first sight, the intimations of the Divine Person behind and above them, find here an echo or a place. Nothing breaks the purifying power of the thing and its apparent fatefulness; the apparent determinism of the phenomena and the mentally and emotionally costing character of their investigation—I think the God of all phenomena as of all reality has now given us in these a purifying medium, which as many will and ought to use as have, in the past, striven to use the medium of abstraction alone.

(d) The recollecting of the soul, and its turning back to its own central necessities and dependence upon God, would of course remain exactly as they were, and as absolutely necessary; only the running away from, or minimising, or illogical tacking on of, an occupation with the world around would cease; it would on the contrary have *its normal necessary place* in the very theory of spirituality: and every man would be taught in Retreats, etc., that he must *study or work* at something definite and concrete, not simply to escape the dangers of idleness or to take off the strain of direct spirituality, but because, without them, he will, as we now know and see things, avoid one of the two twin means of growing lowly and pure, and of removing himself from the centre of his (otherwise little) world.

It would be easy, I think, to show how, even still in St. Catherine's day, science represented by such fantastic and anthropocentric conceptions as those of Paracelsus, and scholarship, by such pretentious omniscience as that of Pico della Mirandola, could not as yet be the ready-found purification I think they both can now be easily turned to; and inasmuch as there was an inherent repugnance to all that is particular and concrete, one would have, I think, however carefully and respectfully, to admit that this was and is a confusion or theoretical misconception: for Blondel is surely right at least where he says that the true Absolute and Universal springs for us from the true concrete and particular: God, I like to think with Lotze, is the supremely concrete, supremely individual and particular, and the mental and practical occupation with the particular must ever remain an integral part of my way to Him. And this squares so grandly with the whole sacramental doctrine and practice of the Church. One gets otherwise into a Neo-Platonic depersonalising of the soul.

You will please forgive me: it has profited me, even if you cannot answer much or anything.

Yours ever most gratefully and sincerely,

SL, pp. 72-74   Fr. von Hügel.

In this letter of counsel to his daughter, there is a remarkable piece of self-analysis.

To Hildegard von Hügel   (1899)

I have so long now got to see in myself a certain peculiarity, which the Hügel papers have proved to me to be inherited, and traces of which (in varying forms and degrees) I think are in all three children too, though least in you, I fancy. It is a peculiarity which I was long in seeing in myself, and which will give me *arms*-full, *cart*-loads full of fight and work, as long as I live. It is this. There is, on the one hand, a very real degree of originality, a very genuine requirement of a large liberty, of much initiative and great activity, this is good and should get its food and scope. There is, on the other hand, a strong tendency to fall out of the ranks; to break away from the *corporate*, the belonging, as a part, to any one body as a whole: to be difficult and contrary; to be violent and obstinate; to fret when I cannot get my way;

not ever, fully and frankly to endorse and deliberately, freely *will* those subjections and limitations, those docilities and obedience with which life is so mercifully full. And it took me long before I saw plainly that *this second tendency* is weak and foolish, *is the deadly enemy of the first*; and that I could only be really true and strong, really manly and Christian, inasmuch as I trained myself to love and will, to insert right into my heart, to take up as it were into my very blood and system, the idea and the fact of all such limitations, dependences, obediences, docilities, as God has surrounded and really saved me with.

I do not know to what degree this same point applies to you; but it is sure to apply in *some* degree, if only because you are a human being and young; probably also because you are a Hügel, and in part a daughter of our day which, of course, has its special weaknesses as well as special strengths. And it is a point on which I naturally care to speak out, because it was the keen consciousness within myself both of the need of a large liberty, and the absolute necessity of its being a real docility and true dependence, and the feeling of how easily I (presumably than any one of my children) would jib and rear against it, not simply in the home, but in the Church and everywhere—that made me bring you girls up, so very unhampered, so very freely. Yes, but with it, of course, I had to run the risk for you, that this would be taken not as a *means*, but as an end, not as making docility, and the beautiful attitude of trust and teachableness, of corporate inter-dependence and tendency to agree wherever reasonably possibly, more easy, but as superseding or weakening all these priceless virtues. It might too, of course, so easily be taken as a starting-point for going faster in the same direction, whereas it was considered from the first, but as forming into a positive hindrance and danger if pushed further afield. And I have, of course, seen with my own eyes, this danger become actual for a while, tho' not in your case. Darling daughter, see carefully to it that such danger as you may find in your case, never becomes a reality, never gets broken down under.

I have had to train myself away from all unnecessary discussions, from all too long or too detailed or constant criticism of others. Even so, I often weaken myself by this fault, and I am trying to practise that most strengthening thing: to take, in cases where I am not called upon to judge or help, just the good and true that I can and do see, and to not judge, not criticize the rest. In this way one can more easily keep and strengthen the immensely important habit of looking up to people, feeling oneself their inferiors and learners.

B, pp. 117–118

George Tyrrell is in difficulty as a member of the Society of Jesus and von Hügel begins his counseling that will continue over the next ten years in an attempt to keep Tyrrell's inward life strong as he faces the outer trials that are to come to him.

To George Tyrrell   (*March 4, 1900*)

My dear Father Tyrrell,

I feel more than usually sorry and guilty at having left your kindnesses so long unacknowledged; for you have been in trouble, and a word of sympathy from one's friends—though it is no cure—is yet—who has not himself experienced it?—a very precious gift of God. But I know well that you will have felt sure how entire and constant my sympathy is with your work and ideal, with what you have done (so quite astonishingly much) and with what you would do and still do (so much more again). I can say in all simple truth that, since Newman's death, there has been no English-speaking Catholic whose work appeals to me, and pierces, I think, to the very centre of questions, to a degree at all really comparable to yours. And *your* trouble has, hence, been most really *my* trouble also. Accustomed as I am, for now well-nigh thirty years, to find my friends and helpers having to scud before the gale, or to lie low and spend a good part of their life and strength in avoiding, parrying, or anticipating blows—I was still hoping that *you* might somehow, with the (temporary) loss of your professorship of now some years ago, have paid your price, and that no further check would come. Still, considering everything, we have even now much cause for gratitude and unbroken trust for, after all, it has only come *now*; and, even now, it is more trying than destructive, even, I take it, for the moment.... Without an active, carefully fostered spiritual, mystical life and habit of mind, a hungering and thirsting after what is above and beyond the power of all the natural or indeed any sciences to awaken or to supply—a man remains or becomes but half a man, uninteresting and vulgar (even simply intellectually), and of course ceases to have all patience with the imperfect administration, and even all tenderness for the real requirements and duties, of a religion which has ceased to stimulate and to supply a faculty and want of his nature. . . .

VHT, pp. 123–127

His daughter Gertrud is again the subject of a letter to Tyrrell. The reference to Catherine of Genoa and to his work on her refers to a labor that began with a brief article in 1896 and ended in 1908 as a great two-volume classic of religious philosophy which William Temple predicted would be the most important book in that field published in England during the first half century.

To George Tyrrell   (*4 Holford Road: July 7, 1900*)

Since I saw you, or even wrote you, I have had a fresh proof and instance as to how living a substance the soul is,—maintaining its life always by a continual re-constitution, by effort, strength, temptation, growth, and new levels and starting-points, although all this is, no doubt, the case in very varying degrees and forms amongst various souls. But the greater the soul, the greater such development. I am feeling it with and for a much prized, closely watched soul, that is evidently, please God, moving on to another, a higher level, but all the perplexity and danger of the transition : please pray for her. And I am observing it in my working at St. Catherine : it is simply comical to note the divergence between the *facts* of her continuous struggle, effort, and changing, growing achievements and horizons, and her biographer's emphatic insistence, at every halt in her life, or even of his narrative, that *now* at last (he has said so, as absolutely as language permits, of even the first moment of her conversion) she is at the very summit of perfection.

SL, pp. 86–87

In order to comfort his impetuous Irish friend, George Tyrrell, he passes on this somewhat stoical but profound piece of wisdom from his old friend Abbé Duchesne, the great church historian.

To George Tyrrell   (*August 19, 1900*)

. . . years ago, Duchesne said to me, and I have so often found him right, in the lives of my various friends and my own :

Work away in utter sincerity and open-mindedness; lead as deep and devoted a spiritual life as you can; renounce from the first and every day, every hope and wish for more than toleration; and then, with those three activities and dispositions, trust and wait with indomitable patience and humility, to be tolerated and excused. You will find that if only you have patience and magnanimity enough to wait so long, and to work so hard, and to put up with apparently small result—*that* result will not fail you : you will be put up with, not more, not one inch more : but *that* much you *will* achieve.

VHT, pp. 130-131

Maude Petre was a gifted woman writer on religion who eventually became George Tyrrell's close spiritual friend and protector, and at his death, his literary executor and biographer. In his letters to her as in those to Tyrrell, von Hügel's accent on the relative independence of the external world in which we have been placed and of its role in quickening the deepest levels in us if we do not try to shun it, is conspicuously to the fore.

To Miss Maude Petre   (*4 Holford Road: September 26, 1900*)

He (God) intends to help us only to make our own selves, and gives us to begin with our materials but not the results, and *never, at any time, in the materials practically, the results already.* You and I will, in a most real sense, be tomorrow different, fuller or lesser, and truer or falser, Personalities than we are to-day, and this not simply automatically, but entirely through the more or less deliberate acts and acceptances of our volitional nature, and the countless effects and habits of its past volitional history as thus now again endorsed or revoked, and the grace of God working in and through these our acts that will take place within the next twenty-four hours. We shall be passing out of the light, the fact of what we are at this moment, through the right or wrong contraction, the darkness and the effort of the right or wrong act, out into the fresh and fuller, or the more dead and dimmer new light. . . . What God is in Himself we, strictly speaking, do not know. All our true knowledge of Him is limited to what He is to us and in us. And this knowledge is necessarily not at the beginning but at the end of our struggles and endeavours, since it grows with the growth of our own personality, ever the joint work of ourselves and God.

We cannot, I am persuaded through and through, show our apprehension of the secret of His law of spiritual life for us all, or cooperate in building it up, better than in ever remembering, ever vividly realising, ever practising, ever suffering the (within our world of relativities) *true and real independence* which God has chosen to give Creation, by the very fact of creating it, and still more by incarnating Himself in its head and centre, man. Never, as truly as creation will never be absorbed in the Creator, nor man, even the God-man, become (or become again) simply and purely God, will or can science and art, morals and politics be without each their own inside, their own true law of growth and existence *other than, in no wise a department or simple dependency of, religion.* The creature is not the Creator, either in quantity or quality, it is not a little god; and yet, though it is indefinitely lesser, the Creator respects its inferior and different nature. Even so are science and all the other departments of life not religion, or to be absorbed in it, or to be anything but as scrupulously reverenced by religion.

And this is immensely difficult to the natural man. For the very minute you have a deep and vivid religion, that very minute you have, almost irresistibly, the omnipresent conviction that either *religion is everything,* since it is admittedly the most important and most universal of all things; and doesn't the greater ever include the lesser; or, at all events, that, if the other departments require religion, religion does not require them.

All this would actually make him seek and postulate, in such a moral training school, just precisely the friction, the non-fit, the *otherness* of science and of religion, of the phenomenal determinism, and the noumenal libertarianism; just exactly that scheme of things in the midst of which we are: in our foreground ourselves, selfish, sensual, childish individuals, mere *units,* but with the mysterious capacity (not more!) for constituting ourselves unselfish, spiritual, manly personalities, real unities and organisms; in the middle distance, the phenomenal curtain and, as it were, buffer-state, the resisting, but spiritually not irresistible, medium of the world of physical, mechanical, determinist fact, law and science; in the background, which is really the ground-work also of all, the noumenal reality, the world of spirits and of the absolute Spirit, of persons and the absolute Person, the world of liberty, morality, eternity and love. . . . Only through this friction, admitted, recognised, fully and carefully retained, will our soul be able to rightly and richly move on and grow and become. . . . Hence religion will have to come to see that it cannot attain to its own depth, it cannot become the *chief thing,* if it does not continually renounce to aspiring after being *everything;* for it cannot become its own fullest self without, not merely occasioning the love of the Cross in other departments, but also taking the Cross upon *itself.* And then all things will become food for such a faith, and it will become the base, and transfigurer of all things.

P.S. The day on which the Christian ascetical spirit shall have woken up to the *irreplaceable* value for it of *the thing*, of a preliminary *fatalism*, on that day will the good man, because he wants to be better, wish to be not 'clever,' God knows; not 'learned,' God knows again : but he will have a horror of ignoring these bitter waters, prepared by God Himself to bring death to his merely natural, petty anthropomorphism, and will have done for good with all deliberate hankering after a juxtaposition of Faith and Science.

SL, pp. 89–96

To George Tyrrell   (*Milan: December 18, 1901*)

I can most truthfully declare that no day passes, but you are at least thrice definitely in my prayer; as you are one of that little band, scattered throughout space, but united, I feel happily confident, in its struggles, prayers, and ideals, which ever cheers me on, to try and do better, to give more really all, gratefully, and to accept the *something* that comes of it. I find lots more has to stand over.

Your very affectionate friend,

VHT, p. 100   F. von Hügel.

To George Tyrrell   (*June 4, 1902*)

If then I was asked to sum up the upshot of my mind of the impressions of the last six weeks, I would say that it comes to this: the world is wide and rich, complex and difficult, my masters. The battle in it, the struggle upwards and inwards of life and light is slow, varied, often checked and thrown back. Those that try and push matters on must be prepared, more or less, for martyrdom. But, oh joy, things move, things grow, light comes, and souls are helped, for all that, and all that, and not one pang, or sigh, or tear of the labourers or the self purifiers is lost or fails to go directly to help on this increase of life for souls. Work, work away at your German, *mind*, and please!

Your very affectionate old friend,

B, p. 141   F. von Hügel.

Here von Hügel speaks to an Anglican professor friend of the greatest gift he finds in the Roman Catholic Church : its capacity to produce saints; but in the same breath he puts the force in the

Roman Catholic Church that must be purged from within if a spirituality of the open type exemplified in a Nicholas of Cusa is to return.

To Professor Percy Gardner   (4 Holford Road: April 25, 1903)

I see a double phenomenon, of another sort, on the other side. I see, it is true, and I rejoice in the sight, that countless souls have been and are deeply, spiritually Christian, in every form of Protestantism. Yet I cannot but note that Catholicism, *at its best*, still somehow produces saints of a depth of other-worldliness, of a delicate appealing heroism, and of a massiveness of spiritual wisdom, greater than I can find elsewhere. And indeed I note that men so much outside our system as William James are generally ready enough to admit this. . . . I was so much struck with the keen insight of our Bishop Spalding of Peoria, U.S.A. (whose family have been American for 200 years), when, in Rome three years ago, he developed before me with astonishing eloquence the contention, that history had conclusively manifested and established two things; the impossibility, for any society and state that would live and grow, of the Spanish, physical force, sheer authority, and blind obedience type of Catholicism; and the incapacity of pure Protestantism, e.g., the Free Churches of America, to produce the very deepest and largest saints. Hence the future seemed to him and to myself to demand the legitimate aspirations and the undoubted benefits of Protestantism should be realised and should remain, and that corresponding changes should occur from within, in the attitude and practice of Catholicism; . . .

SL, p. 120

A signal service of von Hügel to the Christian religion in Britain was to underline the transcendent element in religion at a period when idealistic immanentism, 'God in us', had swept the field.

To George Tyrrell   (May 30, 1903)

Your letter has given me far more pleasure than I can adequately describe or at all requite, in the midst of the final odds and ends, before decamping, till Thursday, to Cambridge. For you have evidently dwelt upon the *one* idea and conviction in my paper, which I myself feel to be of certain and abiding importance. I have had for years, increasingly, a double sense: of the large, spacious, range of our ethical etc. capacities, and of the necessity and value of an ideal and indefinite exercise for them; *and* of all this not being God, not one bit, not one bit. . . . God is emphatically *not* simply our Highest Selves; heaven for us will *not* be a simple adequation or a simple identification (even in *kind*, apart from all degree) of our nature with God's; religion is *not* a simple or full intercourse between equals (in kind any more than in degree), where the movement from God to man can be understood by tracing it backwards, in the movement from man to God. All Universal Exhibition,—Prince Albert-and-dear-Bunsen 'religion'; all Mechanics' Institutes—or British Empire—or other human-ideals prolonged, purified, enlarged indefinitely, can, at best, but help us to get nearer to a sense of that difference, in and through our own enlargement. I am hot, weary stupid : I am longing for my holiday, and must think no more.

SL, pp. 124–125

To George Tyrrell   *(April 30, 1904)*

Endless patience; the knowledge of when to yield and bend, and when and where to hold out; and meanwhile the opposing in oneself of that sorry weakness which would pay back one's own sufferings, either at the expense of the great cause or by that last refuge of defeat—cynicism, . . . these things I feel I must practise at constant cost. . . . But what is life, all moral, spiritual, rational—and Christian and Catholic life and reform in self and others—but *that?*

VHT, p. 152

There is instruction in the way the counselor himself faces the interruptions which life sends him. The word that man's interruptions can be God's opportunities is not a mere copy-book maxim for von Hügel.

To George Tyrrell   *(June 30, 1904)*

My very dear Friend,—Had I the time, I could and would write a series of long letters, instead of this scrappy note. Never mind : we shall soon, thank God, be meeting, for a good long time. Hence now I only jot down unadjournable items.

(1) As Miss Petre will have told you,—Archbishop Mignot is coming to stay with us here, on the 15th or 16th, for 10 days : and I much wish you could and would come up to town to see him. I am planning two nights for him at Oxford,—arriving there for lunch on one day, and leaving after breakfast two days

after, for Cambridge, probably, for one night. And this excursion is likely to take place during the middle of his stay,—say on July 20-23rd. So, if you come up, it would have to be for before or after, or for before *and* after, those days. Think favourably of the plan, please. . . .

This is all a distinctly costing affair for me,—it means ten precious days clean taken out of my work: and deafness means crippledness and a handsome crop of little humiliations during such social attempts. The book meanwhile is really getting on again: but I want to abstain from all forecasting of time: labour, prayer, and as much serenity and cheerful toil as I can manage and God will give me: and the rest will find its own level.

Your very affectionate Friend,

SL, pp. 127-129   Fr. von Hügel.

Speaking to Maude Petre of Tyrrell's situation if he were to leave the Society of Jesus and to leave behind all the duties that it laid down for him, he counsels caution on the alleged freedom that this would bring.

To Maude Petre   *(September, 5-7, 1905)*

I feel so strongly what an immense help it is to my own soul's health and growth that I am not free to fix the degree or kind of my relations with my fellows, but that the chief of them are all determined for me—as son, brother, husband, father and hence I cannot but wistfully regret that if and when he leaves the S. of J. he will have next to none of the priest's substitutes for such fixed mutual obligations. . . . I too have much experience of the way in which much steady work acts as an anodyne: indeed I think that next to prayer and alongside of the open air and physical exercise, it is the most infallible of helps—But I pray God that your troubles and anxieties may soon be lessened. I too have two or three big trials upon me—so I can thoroughly understand and sympathize. Please, please pray for me and these situations. I do so for you every day.

MSS. of v. H. Correspondence
in British Museum.

Tyrrell was separated from the Society of Jesus in 1906 and his spiritual counselor is warning him against the too easy way of counter-attack. He is also guarding religion against the reductionist tendencies that were springing up in some quarters of the modernist ranks.

To George Tyrrell (*December 18, 1906*)

Already these two positions are absolutely unworkable unless we are willing and perseveringly determined slowly and deliberately to let drop, to damp down, as far as possible to exterminate, cleverness as distinct from wisdom, clearness as distinct from depth, logic as distinct from operativeness, simplicity as distinct from life. Nothing is easier than unconsciously to retain the ultramontane *Fragestellung,* and then to answer this with the most contemptuous negative; nothing is more readily achieved than to take, say, Cardinal Merry as the true, sincere type of Catholic and to show that none of our group are, then, Catholics at all. Indeed the thing is so easy, that quick-witted men like Houtin ought to feel somewhat ashamed of their apparent pride and pleasure in pointing out something so glaringly obvious. That I for one cannot go along this path; and that much getting into the open air, much (largely) informal prayer, and much persevering hard work, in combination, bring me, in my best moments, to a frame of mind where all the deepest, truest, alone really fruitful work and insight in these greatest things, appears as achieved in this sort of but approximately 'logical', obtuse-seeming, costingly wise, not brilliantly clever, ruminant, slow, if you will, stupid, divinely blest, thorn-crowned, ignored, defeated, yet soul-inspiring, life-creating fashion. . . . A very peaceful, fruitful Christmas to you, valiant friend, who have done so much : so much that even your great sufferings and trials have not been,—thank God,—too great a price.

SL, pp. 136–137

To George Tyrrell (*October 1, 1907*)

[In a postscript to the letter :]

So deeply sorry for all your pain and worry;

So deeply grateful for all that is so great and deep in your present work and writing;

So entirely understanding, thank God, even where I feel certain limitations and imperfections. Even if these latter be really there,—God will, from our sufferings and good intentions, build up something that will include all our gold and exclude such dross as may here and there depreciate it.

SL, p. 142

To George Tyrrell (*November 15, 1907*)

A dominant hatred and determination to destroy even a set of men or an institution predominantly evil: such a disposition would, the writer of this scribble is absolutely certain, shrivel up and evaporate all the true power, all the deep glorious helpfulness of G.T., long before he had done any serious execution upon those his enemies. May G.T. keep realising this, and that we have no opponents who can do us or our cause much harm, except in this our temptation, our weakness, which might drive us into such sterilising negation and feverish hate.

Devoted old friend,

SL, p. 145 Fr. von Hügel.

To Maude Petre (*13 Victoria Gate, Kensington, W.,
February 20, 1906*)

I have, of course, been greatly appreciating those seven or more weeks of practically daily intercourse with Fr. T.; and your sister's kind hospitality was, I am sure, greatly appreciated by him. I think that the point concerning his own happiness and efficiency which most impressed itself, again and perhaps more than ever, upon me, was his unappeased craving for just that kind of activity which he had when giving Retreats, Conferences, and trusted by and helping souls as a Catholic Priest and Religious. I think too that he feels the want of this activity also in view of writing. He said one day, quite 'off his own bat': 'all this controversial, Church-political, newspaper writing makes one empty and bitter. I long to get back to mystical ways and mystical subjects, and yet I cannot, I am out of tune for them. And I cannot sit down and write a spiritual book in cold blood: I have never done so, and could not do so now.' I hope, however, that slowly he will learn to make the very most of a slowly increasing informal very real pastoral activity among men and women, young and older of all sorts; and that with this stimulation and with the peace of Storrington, he will be able to set to the writing of another more or less devotional or religious psychology sort of book; and that this occupation will in its turn, react upon him in a bracing, soothing, expansive manner. Already I see traces of things working in this direction with him. I *am* so glad.

MSS. of v. H. Correspondence
in British Museum.

above all, I insisted strenuously upon how he should not let his mind dwell upon securing, *at any price*, the greatest help towards perfection, but should, on the contrary, directly aim only at making the best of his situation, and not think of leaving it short of plain and peremptory admonitions of his own conscience that, in thus remaining, he was committing positive and grievous sin. That as long as he strove thus, with all his heart and with ever increasing prayer and dependence upon God's grace, he would gain, even where he would seem to be losing. And that this would not involve the not profiting by our best books, and such help as he might feel drawn to seek from spiritual but unproselytising Catholics. I lent him the two vols. of Fénelon's *Spiritual Letters*, and Grou's *Manuel*. I was sorry to find that he knows not one word of French, even for reading purposes.

SL, pp. *162–163*

Here the realism and the transcendent aspect of religion are distinguished from morality into which men are forever trying to reduce it.

To Malcolm Quin   (*November 17, 1909*)

You appeal with A.C., to righteousness, to the hunger for moral perfection, as the easy, true, way to religion, and Catholicism,—and this as though there were an identity between morality and religion. I should answer; 'for propaedeutic purposes, yes; intrinsically, no.' I feel confident that the two are not, *at bottom*, the same thing, nor even different stages of the same thing. And further it appears to me that it is the insistence upon some such identity which gives Comtism (in spite of its intellectual breadth, fine *moral* fervour, and its touching reverence for Catholic forms of religion) a (to my feeling) curiously heavy, opaque, *doctrinaire* 'feel' and tone, when it is simply itself and talks religion. Religion, I feel more and more, is (in contrast with Ethics) essentially concerned with what *already is* and most speedily will be, and with what is indeed environing and penetrating man ever on and on, but yet as super-human, other than simply human, as truly transcendent, and not only immanent. I think that A. E. Taylor in his *Problem of Conduct*, and others have recently brought into striking prominence this '*is*-ness' of religion, as against the '*Ought*-ness' of morals. And certainly I have noted, more and more, how distinct, how rarely developed *pari passu*, are the religious intuition and the moral sense. A whole procession of figures is passing before my mental vision at the moment possessed of keen ethical sense, and with little or no religious instinct; and then, a much smaller set of souls, aglow with the specific religious sense, and having little or no specially *moral* awakeness. And hence I cannot but think that a religion without God, does not correspond to the specific religious sense, because no amount of *Oughtnesses* can be made to take the place of one *Is*-ness.

SL, p. 174

Chapter II

SPIRITUAL LETTERS: 1910-1918

T HE letters to J.M. (Juliet Mansel), the 17-year old grand-daughter of one of his devoted friends, show again the Baron's extraordinary genius for taking infinite pains in the spiritual guidance which he shared with this young girl.

To J.M. (a Girl at School)   *(March 23, 1910)*

I was so grieved on finding out last Sunday that we had missed your birthday. Even though, this time a bit late, I am sending you, by this post, a little birthday present. I have chosen for you Boswell's *Life of Johnson*, in the best smallish-sized one-volume edition now on the market, because, though parts of it are dull (so are parts of Homer, Shakespeare, Milton, even of the Bible), it contains, in quite three-fourths of its bulk, things that have not died and will never die. I hope you may end by feeling, with me, Johnson to be a true help towards serving God, towards that inner life without which we are empty and poor indeed. And so I give you the book, as one more proof of my prayerful trust that it is not with you a silly child's passing whim, a shabby senti-mentality of the 'salad' years, but a simple, humble determina-tion, with God's grace, quietly and wisely, with much breadth and ever renewed patience, to constitute yourself, on and on, into a spiritual personality. I feel, somehow, a happy trust that you will never, permanently at least, add the pang, to so many others, of your ending in the mere drift and fever of the surface, faddy, selfish life—so near to the best of us, as long as we are here below.

I also want to say, Child, that I should like you to-morrow (Maundy Thursday) to mind and read those most glorious *verses 1-17 of Chapter 13 of St. John's Gospel.* I should like you to read and pray over them *very* carefully—thinking how *you* are called

to wash your neighbors' feet—the feet of those God has specially given you. And on *Good Friday*, I should like you to read
similarly

Imitation Book III. c. xxvii
and Book IV. cc. viii, ix.

I have striven to work that *St. John* and these *Imitation* glories
slowly, thoroughly, into my poor man's life. You will similarly
strive, but patiently, sensibly, practically, to work them into
yours. Of course, only prayer and dependence upon God, and a
cheerful humility which will learn how to learn, and be grateful
for little buffets and humiliations, has any *chance* even of perseverance. To-morrow will be half-way to the joy of our having
you here. It will be with a very shout of joy that this old Father-
thing will welcome you here. And meanwhile careful work,
entering gratefully into everything, School, play, leisure, sleep,
etc., as if each, as it comes, were the one only thing in the world.
Without such variety, no wholesome growth, religious or otherwise. Oh how grateful I am to God for this schooling of yours!
How precious are these months! Love them, browse among
them, bid them, were it possible, to tarry! They will found you
for life, for love, for the happy service and growth in and for
God and man.

SL, pp. 175–176

To J.M.   (*May 24, 1911*)
The fact is that the poor thing that scribbles these lines is the
work of religion. I weigh my words, Child: I should not be
physically alive at this moment, I should be, were I alive at all,
a corrupt or at least an incredibly unhappy, violent, bitter, self-
occupied destructive soul were it not for religion—for its having
come and *saved me from myself*—it, and nothing else; it, in place
of everything else, it, in a sense even against everything else, I know
well how many, probably better-natured people there are in the
world who seem never to have felt this; I know how many others
there are who *seem* to feel it, but who do not really, not enough,
at least, to determine their lives; and keenly do I realise *how*
many, *how* grave are the problems and difficulties that spring
up with and in religion, and how carefully, patiently, devotedly,
they require to be met *au fur et à mesure* of their turning up,
unless the soul is to be thrown back. But, I also know beyond

argument or a moment's hesitation, that my experience is absolutely not an eccentric one; and that, in the long run and upon the whole, humanity itself *realises* that it cannot do without religion, and that even when and where it does not realise this, it is the less deep, the less tender, the less completely true without it. But then, as Miss Alice Gardner, in a good talk with me, once said, when reflecting upon her experiences of religious indifference among some (but now decreasingly numerous) girls now-a-days, the difficulty to get people to see the need of religion lies in this, that many people really *have* got naturally fairly harmonised 'good', i.e., not violent, not passionate, not neck-or-nothing natures; and that such people, if they live in a predominantly non-religious age, can live and die with little or no religion, without coming to grief in *tangibly* immoral ways, or without finding *clearly* that they are miserable in themselves if left to their own unaided resources. And the damage of the non-religion to such souls, she thought, not they themselves, but only very spiritual people, could see.

Well now, as long as souls are in *that* condition or of *that* sort, *religion has, as a matter of fact, no genuine entrance into them;* and religious friends, those to whom religion is their life, could very easily, I think, even do harm, for they might, by offering wares for which there is no conscious wish, simply irritate or strain, by so doing.

I feel as though you are now getting thoroughly awake, Child, as though you sincerely long to fight, to drop, to overcome self. Without that dividing up of the true self against the false, without a fear and dread of self that will drive you to God and Christ, without a taking in hand daily, and ever humbly beginning anew, but *not in your own strength, but in a despair of self,* which, if true, means *an utter trust in God and Christ,* so utterly near you day and night,—religion is fine talk, at least it has not become fully alive; and without such a life as *that,* Child,—note what I say—you will *never* be happy, you will become feverish, bitter, hard, odious, or will shrink into a poor surface-thing— although I doubt whether you could, whether God would let you achieve the latter.

Even now I feel a little fear as if I were somewhat previous with all this. For are you not only turned 18? And are you not going to have a little fun? And why be so solemn and so serious with but a child, with but a girl.that should be treated slightly, or at least considered to be a thing that will run through a

thousand moods before she has done, and not as one to be en-
trusted with the deepest most sacred truths and trusts given to
suffering, toilsome men? Yet I cannot believe this, even though
one's contrary faith, *like every faith of any worth and use*, contains an element of risk, of creative trust *that cannot be proved*
right before the event. I see you *a soul capable of being, oh,*
so miserable, so violent, so bitter, fierce, hard, self-destructive.
I know you to be now at years and even months, which will
build up in you either the right or the wrong habits or drifts.
And I see, with joy, that just the necessary, the *unique* foundation for all those habits is there, doubtless laid by God. I could,
of course, try to help you to find peace, just simply in your non-
combatted self, in the exclusion of the deeper promptings of the
religious sense. Yet *not what you give will make you suffer, in*
the long run, but what you keep back; not the fear and hatred
of self, but all temporising with it. Every self-conquest will mean
peace. Of course I am aiming at no new practices, at nothing
you do not already know well. But *these* would be the chief
points, I think, for your examination of conscience, for turning
over at Spiritual reading, and for your little silent cries to God,
in your recollection, during the day.—(1) dropping quietly all
favourable comparison of self with others, indeed all unnecessary
self-occupation, all self-sufficiency, all self-completeness; (2) putting in place of all *that*, love, service, adaptableness, attention to
occupation with others, *ever so much, to the verge of weakness;*
and (3) above all, continuous, infinite, tenderness, devotedness to,
trust in, service of the darling Mother, doing your little season-
ing with, *and in fullest union with her*, with love, you understand, love, Child, *love*! Mind, now, no naturalism, no goodness
in your own strength. Pretty rotten rubbish that would be.

   God bless you, Child mine. Pray for me.

  SL, pp. 188–189

   In writing to Emilia Fogelklou (Norlind), he once again reiterates
the need of the institutional and of the 'non-religious contingencies'
but makes clear to her the infinite variety of souls there are and of
how aware a guide of souls must be of this fact if he is not to fail
them.

To Emelia Fogelklou   (*January 11, 1911*)
   When that very noble-hearted, deeply religious, utterly un-
worldly friend of mine, W. G. Ward, 'Ideal' Ward, who had been

a Broad Church Anglican, a disciple of Thomas Arnold, Head-
master of Rugby School, had *next* been a puseyite—an ardent
follower of J. H. Newman—and had lastly not only become a
Roman Catholic, but one of the advanced guard, one of the chief
leaders and makers of latter-day Ultramontanism—that is of
pretty well all the miseries the Roman Church is now acutely
suffering from : when this eager, one-sided, great, unintentionally
unjust, soul was dying, he told his second son that, looking back,
he now saw that the main error and mischievousness of his life
consisted in his *having ever more or less assumed that all souls
were of the pattern of W. G. Ward's*, that, wherever God's grace
really worked upon a real good will, it would use the same
means, it would result in the same kind and degree of, not only
spirituality but theology as his own. And that now, face to face
with death, he saw how *endlessly manifold were souls as made
by God*, and how *various were the degrees and kinds of light and
aid given by Him*. Now I have felt called upon by my conscience,
and I think, my increasing knowledge of souls, to keep a careful
watch upon myself not to fall into a mistake analogous to that
of W. G. Ward's. I say 'analogous', because my own mind and
attrait are very distinct from his, so that, if I allowed myself to
be *closed*, I would be shut up against other kinds of souls than
were those which W.G.W. misjudged.

I venture to think that souls of a mystical *attrait*, as I know
is mine, and as I do not doubt is yours, *have a very special need
of the reminder I have ventured thus to put before you*. For such
souls will not only find the contingent *in religion*, the historical,
and the institutional, the *hic et nunc*, the spatial and temporal,
an irritation and an (apparent) oppression and limitation; they
will also tend to find, in so far as they are dominated by their
specific religious *attrait*, all the other *non-religious contingencies
and activities* of man's life, a weariness and an irritation. Why
the Hebrew articles—with God ever present? Why the Greek
accents with His Spirit ever speaking? Why the geography of
the Holy Land? Why particular prayers, why any oral prayers
at all? Yet, look you, please, all the feeling, can only be *one*
element, *one* movement, *one* side of the full truth.

For God is an immense *concretion*, not an abstraction. He is
a *multiplicity* (for our apprehension) *in unity*. He has 'gone *out
of Himself*' by love, and shows His nature supremely in His
attention and care for every sparrow; He has come down to man,
He has given Himself no doubt everywhere, yet in *different*

degrees and ways; He is *not equally* in Jesus and in Nero, He is *not equally* in Nero and a mad dog. He has made my body and its senses, He has made my love of the historical, social, institutional, even the legal; I am to *incarnate*, in my turn, the *incarnate* God; I am not only to express spirit in and through matter, I am also to awaken, and cause to grow, and to purify (by the painful contraction and friction involved) by my contacts with, by my give and take, this my spirit from, and to, matter. No floating, no drifting, no dreaming above the body, the family, society, history, institutions, but a penetrating into them, and a retiring out from them, again to return *Antaeus-like*, to earth.

B, pp. 253–254

To the Rev. Canon Newsom   (*September 21, 1911*)

I trust too that, sooner or later, you may specially like what I have been groping after in the last chapter,—the purgatorial function of severe scientific method and habits, within the complete life, with regard to religion as, at first and ever readily, lived by empirical man. Tyrrell considered that I had there got hold of a fact and principle which have a large future before them. May I, or others, succeed in making it clearer and more impressive.

SL, p. 192

To J. M.   (*October 13, 1911*)

I tell you, my Blessing, because, do you know, I see more and more clearly how *you* (I say *you*, for we have no responsibilities for others, and others may be, so often are, very different from ourselves) *can never be happy without religion.* And by religion I mean not some vague sentiment, or some beautiful thought, not even, though this is getting nearer to it, moral striving as apart from faith in, and realisation of, the great Spiritual Reality, God, in Whose presence, and Whose will, we thus strive to grow and be : but by and in self-donation, such self-commitment to a, to *the* Reality other than, yet immensely near to, ourselves.

SL, p. 194

To F. M. Connell   (*December 13, 1913*)

And I have been so hard-worked that, for this kind of reading, I can only find my usual quarter of an hour, which has to go to those few books (Bible, and *Imitation*, and *Confessions*) which have been my staple spiritual food hitherto.

SL, p. 203

Edward Talbot, Bishop of Winchester, was an Anglican whom he had known since the days of the Synthetic Society in 1896. Here with the first World War hard upon them, von Hügel states the full depth dimension of religion's distinctive task.

To Bishop Edward Talbot   (*Rome: March 20, 1915*)

I felt it strange that W[illiam]. T[emple]. there so little realised, so little stressed, the primary end and function, surely, of every Church deserving of the august name—the awakening souls to, the preparing them for, the holding before them embodiments of, *the other life*, the life beyond the grave. Very certainly, the Church has also to help in the amelioration of *this life*; but I submit, always after, and in subordination to, and penetrated by, that metaphysical, ontological, other-worldly sense and life which alone completes and satisfies fully awakened man. And only thus shall we be in a position to be fair to the Church's work in the past; for the first object and range of this her care and labours will, and ought to be, distinct from and beyond social improvements. Here . . . the Dean of St. Paul's sees refreshingly clearly.

SL, p. 220

Von Hügel's eldest daughter Gertrud had died in Rome on August 12, 1915 and a further level of his faith is disclosed in this letter to his old friend Maude Petre.

To Maude Petre   (*September 14, 1915*)

Time flies so, that we have already passed the month's mind of that darling child's going to God. And I owe you, all this time, warm thanks for your short, but pregnant and most kind, letter of condolence. But not only was the fortnight, that we remained on in Rome after her going, brimful of things to do, mostly saddening or dreary, yet all things which could not be put off: also this our first fortnight at home, has been one in which it was difficult to write. True, I have written a good many letters, but all have been of sympathy with some of the appallingly large number of people struck, directly or indirectly, by the War, or letters of communication of our own trouble to the few people who, though caring, were not likely to hear of it without such direct telling. Also I have been and am weary,—I suppose, as the reaction from all those months of waiting and watching.

And yet how ungrateful and unreal it would be, to forget, and not permanently to thank God for, the experiences and the lessons of that time—as to the superiority of the spirit over sense and the body: as to the quite fresh and full power of faith in and love of God; and as to the reality, and (in its central facts and forces) not strangeness, of that full, true life beyond these our earthly sufferings and the grave. I was, too, deeply impressed by, and grateful for, the very marked growth of soul I could not but notice in G. since I had last seen her, nearly three years before. Those deepest gifts and graces, which Father Tyrrell and Abbé Huvelin had so nobly and delicately fostered during her time of strain and relative confusion,—these latter so truly caused by my own too great, my thoughtless leaning upon a woman's mind 23 years my junior, had now blossomed into a most touching, most generous profusion. The note of true childlikeness was in everything she did, thought and felt, especially also in those great and most various sufferings which (a quite unusual thing in this malady) were felt with increasing keenness up to twelve hours before the end....

It was most helpful and bracing to follow her acts on August 5th—just a week before she went. For, at 6 o'clock that afternoon, she asked me whether I thought she was dying—that she was sure all the Drs. and Nurses thought so, but that she herself did not feel like it. I told her, I was sure as to the terrible virulence of the disease; as to the astonishing vitality and capacity for long resistance of her constitution; and (above all) as to our only absolute certainties being the mysterious but full wisdom of God's Will, and the privilege and protection of willing *that* alone....

And thus, in the midst of one's literally irreplaceable loss, there well up springs of water of eternal life; and we can stand most bracingly abashed before God's goodness working in and through her.

SL, pp. 221–223

To the Rev. Canon Newsom   (*October 2, 1915*)

Our dearest eldest daughter—the soul closest to me upon earth in all my intellectual work, plans and trials,—the one, too, that I tried most extensively to help and to make grow—left our poor dim troubled earth on August 12th. She went with a full acceptance and loving devotedness to God's Will, as utterly right and loving, which were all the more supernatural and inspiring for us who watched her so closely, because, as all the Nurses and Doctors declared, there was a vitality within her abundantly sufficient to furnish forth a rich, vigorous existence for another thirty years at least; and because she thus had to leave a husband who, already bereft of both parents, possessed of but one—and a half-witted—sister and of no children, lost his one real human support and utterly devoted companion in her. Next to him, I believe that I myself am the greatest sufferer from this blow; yet her sisters, her brothers-in-law, and her many devoted friends are also deeply feeling the disappearance from their lives of something so immensely alive, warm, and self-oblivious.

Nothing, too, could have been finer than the steady helpfulness, the union of professional competence, human tenderness and supernatural faith and radiance, of those English Nun Nurses, and of their very fine Italian Chaplain. Truly Troeltsch is right,—still, under our very eyes, God, the great Reality, and faith in Him as such, and the Beyond, and real faith in *its* reality are the power and peace of our little human Here and Now.

SL, p. 225

Von Hügel's spiritual counsel on suffering is never opened more movingly than in the next four letters. They are almost a testament of counsel on facing physical suffering.

To a Friend in his last illness   (1916)

I need hardly assure you that your illness—the weakness and pain you are suffering, in their various degrees and kinds of tryingness—that all these things are now very much in my mind and heart. Indeed they remain contantly present before me, even when they have to be in the background of my consciousness.

With our dearest Gertrud we were able, for a considerable time, to hope that God would still give her many a year of life. And you yourself are not yet sixty, or barely that. May God give you yet many a year of life! But quite distinct from the question of the length of her life, was that of the *quality* of it—of the suffering and limitations mingling with, and imposed upon, pretty well all her activities. All these things were a present, indeed a pressing question.

And, looking back now, I am grateful for nothing so much as for this—that, given the suffering and trials which God then sent or permitted, He also soon gave her a light, far more vivid and

continuous than it used to be, and an evergrowing acceptance
and active utilisation of it, as to the place, meaning and unique
fruitfulness of such suffering, thus met (as it were) halfway, in
the mysterious, but most certain, most real scheme of the deepest life and of God.

When we first got to Rome, she was wonderfully plucky and
courageous, 'grinning and bearing', a dear stoic. But then
gradually she became, in this too, more and more sensitively
Christian. The Cross became, not simply a fact, to bear somehow
as patiently as we can, but a source and channel of help, of
purification, and of humble power,—of a permanent deepening,
widening, sweetening of the soul.

It was God's holy Will in *her* case that all this growth should
promptly be for the other life. But it would, of course, in no way
have been less precious had she been allowed to live on here,
thus so greatly deepened and expanded, and rendered so far more
helpful than ever before, and that for many a year.

I put all this to yourself, as I do to myself, because I have long
felt that it is *the apparent sterility of suffering* which adds the
final touch of trial to our pains; and that this appearance is *most
truly* only an appearance. Not, of course, that suffering, simply
of itself, is good or operates good; but that God is more living
and real than all suffering and all sin; and that He can, and will,
and does give concomitant opportunities and graces and growths
to the sufferer, if and when the latter is humble, watchful and
prayerful in such utilisations.

How I wish I could help much, very much, to lessen your
pains, but—I admit—above all, towards their transmutation!
You can and will now help us all a hundred times more than
when you were in health; suffering can be the noblest of all
actions.

Yours affectionately,

SL, pp. 226–227   F. von Hügel.

To the same friend   (*February 28, 1916*)

How wonderful it is, is it not, that literally only Christianity
has taught us the true peace and function of suffering. The Stoics
tried the hopeless little game of denying its objective reality,
or of declaring it a good in itself (which it never is), and the
Pessimists attempted to revel in it, as a food to their melancholy,
and as something that can no more be transformed than it can

be avoided or explained. But Christ came, and He did not really explain it; He did far more, He met it, willed it, transformed it, and He taught us how to do all this, or rather He himself does it within us, if we do not hinder the all-healing hands.

Pray for us all, even just in passing, please. In suffering, we are very near to God.

Your affectionate old friend,

SL, p. 228   Fr. von Hügel.

To the same friend   (*March 6, 1916*)

I have your three letters—all written since I last wrote—all before me; and I want, first of all, to say that you will never, please, take any little delay in answering as the least index of my feelings. I had to toil under much pressure till this last Saturday afternoon—two days ago. And then a chill drove me to bed and to sloppy food till lunch time today, Monday.

But unless I am absolutely prevented by ill-health or work that will not brook any break, I will write to you every Monday late afternoon, unless (or until) you do not find any special help in such frequent letters or for any other reason which you need not ever specify. . . .

As to your spiritual question, my dear . . ., as to how you are, not simply, once for all, at the beginning of all this discomfort and pain, to accept and will it; but (as you most rightly feel, a very different thing) how you are to stand it, to keep on accepting it, day by day, even hour by hour, possibly minute by minute (I mean, as to the proximity of pain to pain, and weakness to weakness): let me suggest to you the following. I take it that *this is precisely the most irreplaceable function and grace of suffering*, when it is at all at its fullest, that we cannot, do what we will, cut a decent figure in our own eyes; that it rises, *emphatically*, beyond a stoic exercise. All we can then do (and how dear and darling this poor little 'all' is then to God!) is gently to drop, gently to try to drop, all foresight whatsoever; to treat the question how we are going to stand this for a month, or a week, or a day, or even an hour, as a little presumption on our part. We cannot really, of ourselves, 'stand' it properly, for half an hour; and God will and does give us His grace to stand it, for as long as ever He chooses, provided we will, according to the intensity of the trial, contract our outlook, to the day, or the hour, or even the minute. God, the essentially timeless, will thus and then help His poor timeful creature to contract time to a point of most fruitful faith and love.

SL, pp. 228–230

To the same friend   *(March 27, 1916)*

Of course, I keep your case, and its necessities and possible helps, well in my mind and in my prayers. And since you continue to press me, so gently yet so firmly, to propose to you *whatsoever* I may believe will or might help you to deepen your spiritual life and fully to utilise the suffering that God Himself is now sending you, I will suggest the two following closer practices and self-examinations. I need not say, that they are both intended simply as rough material, or approximate suggestions for your own experimenting and hewing into shape. I do not even want to hear your impressions upon them,—it all aims solely at the depth of your heart and conscience to help the fullest awakening and purification that God may call you to. Certain it is, that only such a growing, deepening (even if interiorly painful at first) can and will anchor your soul in a peace which not all the possible hurricanes of pain or oppressions of physical weakness can break you away from, really, at all.

I would then, first, get my imagination and reason into the habit, not simply of looking at, and looking for, sin as an offence against God, but of realising and picturing it as *always* (except with hardened grave sinners) *chiefly a shirking of some effort, or loneliness, or pain, etc., attached to a light or commandment as it offered itself to us, or a seeking of some pleasure, relaxation, vanity, etc., attached to the contrary course.* Now the cure,— the only cure,—for such shirking of right pain, and for such seeking of wrong pleasure, is precisely the recovering (more and more deliberately) of what mean shirking and mean seeking. *Pain*—most real pain, which comes ready to our hand for turning into *right* pain—gets offered us by God. Try more and more *at the moment itself*, without any delay or evasion, without any fixed form, as simply, as spontaneously as possible, to cry out to God, to Christ our Lord, in any way that comes most handy, and the more variously the better. 'Oh! Oh! this is real: oh! deign to accept it, as a little real atonement for real sin!' 'Oh, help me to move on, from finding pain so real, to discovering sin to be far more real.' 'Oh, may this pang deepen me, may it help to make me real, real—really humble, really loving, really ready to live or die with my soul in Thy hands.' . . . And so on, and so on. You could end by such ejaculations costing your *brain* practically nothing. The all-important point is, to make them *at the time* and *with the pain* well mixed up into the prayer. . . . Pray for me too, I beg of you.

Your very affectionate friend,

H.

SL, pp. 230–232

His emphasis upon the revelation and the corporate institutional historical carrier of the faith as an indispensable element of religion is fiercely to the fore.

To Professor E. A. Sonnenschein (*April 18, 1916*)

Yet I believe it to be a sheer matter of fact that such 'anonymously' supernatural acts, are, *in the long run and upon the whole*, dependent for their persistence amongst men, upon the great Revealers and Incarnations of the prevenient love of the Other-than-ourselves, the Other-than-all-mere humanity—of God, the utterly Concrete, *the* Reality. And amongst these Revealers and Incarnations, Jesus Christ holds the supreme, indeed a unique, place. . . .

It is childish ingratitude to ignore, or to make little of, this long growth of mediations of all kinds. If souls in good faith, if Quakers, are possible in the real world of humanity with but little *conscious* history and with little or no acceptance of institutions, sacraments, dogmas, this is only possible *because this real world has not always been, has at no time predominantly been, a Quaker world*. It is easy to abstract from, to form a quintessence from, that rich (also historico-institutional) world and reality, given the persistent, operative existence and influence, practically everywhere, of the said world; but it would not simply be difficult, it would be strictly impossible, thus to abstract and to distill without those precious but despised concretions.

SL, pp. 234–235

Claude Montefiore, the great Jewish scholar of his day, was an intimate and much loved friend of von Hügel. Philosophy for von Hügel was always compelled to take account of the facts, and religion and the saints were for him ineradicable and primitive facts.

To Claude Montefiore   *(October 28, 1916)*

Thus, here again, I would carefully guard against theology or even religion dictating to philosophy; but why on earth philosophy cannot, and ought not to, study, analyse and articulate the facts and evidences of the religious sense—if such exist and are offered for its study—I do not see.

SL, pp. 238–239

To Claude Montefiore   *(October 29, 1916)*

I believe, then, that both you and I do not read into, but that we actually find in—you in Judaism, I in R. Catholicism, heroisms, sanctities, spiritualities, etc., which are *actually present in, and which actually spring from,* the deepest life of these several organisms. Judas Maccabee, Rabbi Akiba, Maimonides, Sir Moses Montefiore, your own fine first Wife (I quote only the dead) are *facts*—Jewish *facts*, Jewish *products*, I thank God for them—I do not read them into Judaism, nor do you : we find them there. Similarly Francis of Assisi, Joan of Arc, Las Casas, Abbé Huvelin—they are *facts*, Catholic *facts*, Catholic *products* : I do not read them into Catholicism, nor do you : we find them there, and again, we thank God for them.

SL, p. 250

To the Rev. H. Handley   *(September 14, 1918)*

He (Professor von Hertling) came, I remember, to the conclusion that à Kempis nobly, and still most persuasively, embodies the world-fleeing movement essential to all deep religion, and especially to Christianity; but that Thomas is much less satisfactory as to the other, itself also essential element of all deep, or rather of all complete, religion—the world-seeking, the world-penetrating, element. . . .

And Dr. von Hertling pointed out that it is this double sense, or (rather) this single keen sense of the two-fold movement of the spiritual life which is so cryingly wanted in these our days. And hence that, though à Kempis can and should continue to do us the greatest services in feeding that need of solitude, eternity, the Cross, and God, without which Christianity, in spite of any and of all enlightenment and philanthropy, is a weak, one-sided, shallow thing : yet this same à Kempis requires, at least in part, to be brought to and kept within a more continuously *double-pole* outlook than he usually himself supplies.

SL, pp. 252–253

Von Hügel was shocked at Dr. Pusey's complete absorption in things technically religious and this letter seeks to counsel an inquirer to find religion penetrating all life and to realize that religion needs the tensions of all sides of life in order to keep it deep and whole and beyond mere religiosity.

To the Rev. Frank Wane (*September, 1918*)

Non-religious interests, this strikes me as the most important of the points, in the sense that you have evidently been least awake to it so far. Allow me to tell a story which, ever since it was most vividly told me, over 30 years ago, has been influencing me in everyday's life. A very able mind and much tried conscience, an Oxford friend of mine (a Scotchman) who from his father's Presbyterianism passed through Tractarian Anglicanism into the Roman Catholic Church, and who, though later on he fell away, alas, had, during the years of his R.C. priesthood when I knew him well, a wonderful, most rare, sensitiveness to the genius, the latent spirit and affinities of Catholicism in its purity, recounted the following. As a young man at Oxford he had made a 10 days Retreat under Dr. Pusey, staying all the time under his roof, living the Dr.'s life with him, and becoming saturated with his spiritual temper and affinities. He spoke with deep reverence of him, of that experience I think, at the time of the telling, twenty or more years back—years spent, for the most part, as a R.C. member of a Religious Congregation. Now my friend said that, comparing Dr. P's spirit with that of Rome at its best, he had come to be vividly struck by one deep-down, all-pervading, but not directly theological difference. And that he had come to see with a full finality that *there* was the point in which the Dr. and many of his following were (quite unconsciously) really not Catholic. That Dr. Pusey, at least at the stage of his life when my friend was under him (and seeing Dr. P. also entirely outside of Retreats, etc.) was incapable, or had made himself incapable, or deliberately acted as though he were incapable, of taking any interest in anything that was not directly, technically religious, or that was not explicitly connected with religion. And that this was quite uncatholic, quite unlike the greatest of the Catholic saints, quite unlike the Jesus of the Synoptists, with all of whom God is the God of Nature as of Grace—a God deeply interested—if this be not profane—also in not directly religious things—grace things. Two movements—of attachment and detachment, of particularity and of abstraction, of sense and of spirit, of time and of eternity, of place and of ubiquity, etc.: one thing in and with another thing: only these together yield the full blossom, the richest fruit and fascination of Catholicism. I venture to send you my *Eternal Life*. If you will study pp. 55–81, 101–120, 301–378, my present point will become clearer, I hope.

Yours very respectfully,

F. von Hügel.

SL, p. 254

Chapter III

SPIRITUAL LETTERS: 1918-1922

H E is writing here to his niece, Gwendolyn Greene, an Anglican girl whom he has adopted as a spiritual daughter of his advanced years and to whom he gives of his best treasures in trying to make the Christian faith both plausible and real to her. He makes generous use, it will be noted, of the objective tool of history to lead her into an acknowledgment of the givenness of the Christian religion. The words on fastidiousness appear often in his spiritual counsel. For him they divide paganism from Christianity. Puck was his beloved dog. These next letters disclose the art of the spiritual counselor at its best.

To G. G., a Niece   *(December 11, 1918)*

No letter you will ever write to me shall, please God, ever remain unanswered—shall remain without a reply as careful and complete as I can manage to make it. But you may have to wait a bit, my Niece, I never could write with ease—not on such subjects, where we should never write, speak or think except with *voce di petto*, never with *voce di testa*. And now I am still weak, and empty of brain, hence a further delay.

Let me make *three* or *four points* of your letter; and try to explain these as well as I now can manage.

1. *The gradual preparation for, and God's revelations preceding, His fullest self-revelation in Christianity.*

I am very glad you apprehend and appreciate this great fact— a fact, however, which you will have to learn to apply, not only to the *succession of history*, but also to the *simultaneous* present. What I mean is that, not only was Judaism especially, yet also, in lesser and other degrees, Hellenism, Hinduism, etc., an historically previous preparation by God Himself for the fuller and fullest self-revelation; but this *holds still* of those imperfect, mixed forms and degrees of light, in so far as they still continue distinct in the world. The synagogue here in Bayswater is still, now, on Dec. 11, 1918, a fragmentary but very real revelation of God and, however unconsciously, a very real pedagogue to Christ. The little Mosque at Woking is still, for some souls, a yet more fragmentary, but still real, revelation of God and teacher of truths more completely taught by Christianity.... And nothing of all this means that these various religions are equally true (or false), and that it does not matter to which you belong (provided only you are in good faith). No : in these deepest and most delicate of all matters, even a little more light, more power, more reality—even what *looks* a little—means, and is very, profoundly, much. It all only means, that nowhere does God leave Himself without *some* witness, and without *some* capacity on the part of the soul (always more or less costingly) to respond to, and to execute, this His witness. And, again, that everywhere, the means and the process are from fidelity to the light already possessed (yet often difficult to see owing to the agitations and cowardice of the soul), to further light, which again, in its turn, demands a delicate, difficult fidelity and fresh sacrifices. Yet, with each such fidelity and sacrifice, the peace, the power, the joy, the humble fruitfulness of the soul grow. Always it is a search for expansion and happiness, found in acts gently costly and increasingly exacting.

2. *Only the best attractive to you; and any, every Church, very middling, hence dull, repulsive.* Thus you do not go to country Church services, etc.

The touching, entrancing beauty of Christianity depends upon a subtle something which all this fastidiousness ignores. Its greatness, its special genius, consists, as much as in anything else, in that it is without this fastidiousness. A soul that is, I do not say tempted, but dominated, by such fastidiousness, is as yet only hovering round the precincts of Christianity, but it has not entered its sanctuary where heroism is always homely, where the best always acts as stimulus towards helping towards being (in a true sense) but one of the semi-articulate, bovine, childish, repulsively second-third-fourth-rate crowd. So it was with Jesus himself; so it was with St. Francis, the Poverello; so it is with every soul that has fully realised the genius of the Christian paradox. When I told you of my choking emotion in reading, in St. John's Gospel, that scene of Jesus, the Light of the World (that He is this, is an historic fact), as the menial servant at the feet of those foolish little fishermen and tax-gatherers, what do you think moves me but just that huge life-and-love-bringing paradox, here in its fullest activity? The heathen Philosophies, one and all, failed to get beyond your fastidiousness; only Christianity got beyond it; only Christianity—but I mean, a deeply *costingly* realised Christianity—got beyond it. It is really, a very hideous thing; the full, truly free, beauty of Christ alone completely liberates us from this miserable bondage.

'Well, perhaps yes,' you will say; 'but what am I, here and now, to do?' Do, as to church-going, *nothing but what you already do*. Only be conscientious and regular in going to your Holy Communions, whether in country or town, and in going to Church every Sunday when you are in town. But as to your thinking and speaking, pray ruminate, Niece, over what I have been saying; look out, in your readings, for what confirms it; grow shy of any defence of fastidiousness; pray to God gradually to cure you of it, if and when you come fairly to see it to be a poor, a very poor, thing. You rightly dislike (Walter) Pater's 'affectation'. What I call 'preciousness'. Well, in face of the dread facts of human nature, and of the rich teaching of history, that church-fastidiousness is a sort of Paterism.

3. *What is the precise meaning of Thekla's insistence upon religion as primarily an is-ness, not an ought-ness?*

When ... Thekla says 'religion has primarily to do with is-ness not ought-ness', she means that religion is essentially evidential; that it intimates, first of all, that a superhuman world, a superhuman reality *is*, exists. The first and central act of religion is *adoration*, sense of God. His otherness though nearness, His distinctness from all finite beings, though not separateness—aloofness—from them. If I cannot completely know even a single daisy, still less can I ever completely know God. One of the councils of the Church launched the anathema against all who should declare that God is comprehensible. Yet God too, God in some real senses especially, we can most really know, since, as does even the rose, how much more He? since He deigns to reveal Himself to us. He does so in a twofold manner—vaguely, but most powerfully—in the various laws and exigences of life and of our knowledge of it; and clearly, concretely, in and by the historic manifestations in and through the great geniuses and revealers of religion—the prophets and especially Jesus

Christ. These latter manifestations get thoroughly learnt only in and through the various historical religious bodies. It is through men trained through and through in these schools of religion that all the more solid and sane insights and habits, even of the vague religion, get given most of the point and steadiness which, as a matter of fact, they possess.

4. There is not a line of all the above which has not to be learnt in careful detail, in lowly practice, in humble daily fight with self—in docility and docility, on and on. We will gradually, ruminatingly, get the whole unrolled before us. The all-important point is, I think, at each step to feel how rich, how inexhaustible, how live it all really is! *That* is why I am trying to get such words as 'Rome', 'Athens', etc., to mean a great rich world to you.

Gradually I shall give you more directly religious books to ponder; yet, to the end, these should be made to penetrate and purify a whole mass of not directly religious material and life. God is the God of Nature as of Grace, He provides the meal and the yeast. Let us act in accordance with this, His own action.

SL, pp. 257–261

To G. G.　　　　　　　　　　　　　　　　　*(April 7, 1919)*

I wonder whether you realise a deep, great fact? That souls—all human souls—are deeply interconnected? That (I mean) we can, not only pray for each other, but *suffer* for each other? That these long, trying wakings, that I was able to offer them to God and to Christ for my child—that He might ever strengthen, sweeten, steady her in her true, simple, humble love and dependence upon Him? Nothing is more real than this interconnection —this gracious power put by God Himself into the very heart of our infirmities. And, *it is the Church* (which, *imperfectly* understood, 'dumbs' my bewildered Child)—it is the Church which, at its best and deepest, is just *that*—that interdependence of all the broken and the meek, all the self-oblivion, all the reaching out to God and souls, which certainly 'pins down' neither my child nor this her old groping Father—which, if it 'pins down' at all, does so, really only—even taken simply intellectually—as the skeleton 'pins down' the flesh. What a hideous thing the skeleton, taken separately, is, isn't it? Yet even Cleopatra, when in the splendour of her youth, she had such a very useful, very necessary, quite unavoidable skeleton inside her, had she not?

SL, pp. 269–270

To G. G.   (*May 5, 1919*)

Here I am writing to you, in your new temporary home, looking out of your window, I expect, upon how much of past history recorded in gloriously beautiful monuments, poems in stone! And I am doing as my first act (after an urgent business card) on this my birthday, this my scribble to you. I am, alas! alas! 67 years old to-day! Thus, dear Child—you might almost be my grand-daughter—do I strive to attain to the joy of Princess Colombe, in Browning's touching Play. You remember how she, Colombe, had, up to that her coming of age, always received countless, sumptuous presents—and she had found only pleasure, and less and less pleasure, in such receiving. So then she settled she would receive no gifts at all on this, the first day on which she could order her own life in her own way; but she would herself give and give and give. She felt *that* would bring—not pleasure, but joy, but beatitude. And so it did—Colombe finishes her day radiantly happy.

So then, sit on a footstool here, by me, Daughter; and I will try and give you—not exterior things, but interior things—things that cost one a lot to get, a lot to keep. They are things, indeed, that also cost one a good deal to give—and I can clearly tell you why. Look you, Dear, there is simply *nothing* that one soul can transfer to another soul—even at these souls' best—with the particular connotations, the particular experiences of heart and heart, of blood and breeding, of sex and age, etc., yet it is these particularities which incarnate the convictions of any one soul for that one soul. Any one soul can be fully impressive for another soul, only if that first soul comes out, to the second soul, with its convictions clothed and coloured by those its particularities. And yet the second soul, even if thus impressed—even if it thus wakes up to great spiritual facts and laws—this second soul will at once, quite spontaneously, most rightly, clothe and colour these its new convictions with *its* own special qualities and habits and experiences of thought, feeling, imagination, memory, volition. And so—most really—to try and help on the life of another soul means, Dear, a specially large double death to self on the part of the life-bringing soul. For it means death to self before and in the communication—the life-bringing soul

must, already then, discriminate within itself between the
essence of what it has to say and the accidents, the particularities, which clothe the utterance of this essence; and it must
peacefully anticipate the acceptance *at most* of that essence,
and not of these accidents. And then, after the communication,
this soul must be ready actually to back the other soul in the
non-acceptance even of the essence of the message, if there is
evidence that the other soul is not really helped but is hindered,
at least for the time being, by this essence now offered to it. And,
as already said, at best, *only that essence* can and should be
taken over by this other soul and the light-bearing soul, even
then, must at once be busy helping the less experienced soul to
clothe the newly won essence in clothing free from the ward-
robe of this other soul.

You see, this now, as follows, is the point which, with the
sendings of books which I begin to-day, I hope you may end by
seeing clearly, steadily, in your quite individual manner and
degree. . . .

The church, especially *the* Church in the most definite sense,
the Roman Catholic Church, has, at its worst, done various
kinds of harm, introduced complications and oppressions which,
but for it, would not have been in the world. I know this in a
detail far beyond what you will ever know. But, my dearie, let
us keep our heads; and let us ask ourselves, not whether 'Church'
of any kind does not open the door to certain abuses special to
itself, but, primarily, only whether *as a matter of fact* it has not
been through the Church or Churches that Christianity has
been taught or practised; that Paganism has been vanquished;
that Gnosticism and Pantheism have not carried all before them,
long ago : whether indeed it is not owing to the Church and
Churches—to the organised, social, historical, institutional fact
and tradition, that the most independent-seeming, the most
directly inspired souls, do not draw a large part of the purest of
their conceptions.

SL, pp. 270–272

To G. G.   (*August 7, 1919*)

I cannot exaggerate the gain that I think you will derive from
feeding for years upon the *Confessions* (of Augustine). They
more than any other book, excepting the Gospels and the Psalms,
have taught me—and I believe they will teach you.

SL, p. 279

To G. G.   (*August 18, 1919*)

It is *not* true that all religions are equally true, equally pure, equally fruitful—the differences are, on the contrary, profound. And it is our duty never to level down, never to deny or to ignore God's upward-moving self-revelation, God's *type*-religion. At the same time our ardour requires harnessing to patience, to a meek encouragement of all the smoking flax, all the broken reeds, of our earthly time and comrades, for these are God's *individuals.*

SL, p. 286

His remarks on *packing* put to G. G. the heart of his counsel on the sacrament of the present moment, on taking what comes as an offering to God.

To G. G.   (*September 1, 1919*)

I want this little scribble to reach you on your starting your packing-fortnight. I want to put, very shortly, what has helped myself, so greatly, for now a generation.

Well,—you are going pack, pack and unpack, unpack for a fortnight. What is it that I would have you quietly set your mind and heart on, during that in itself lonesome and dreary bit of your road, Child? Why, *this!* You see, all we do has a *double-relatedness.* It is a link or links of a chain that stretches back to our birth and on to our death. It is part of a long train of cause and effect, of effect and cause, in your own chain of a life—this chain variously intertwisted with, variously affecting, and affected by, numerous other chains and other lives. It is certainly your duty to do quietly your best that these links may help on your own chain and those other chains, by packing well, by being a skillful packer.

Yes, but there is also, all the time, another, a far deeper, a most darling and inspiring relation. Here, you have no slow succession, but you have each single act, each single moment joined directly to God—Himself not a chain, but one Great Simultaneity. True, certain other acts, at other moments, will be wanted, of a kind more intrinsically near to God—Prayer, Quiet, Holy Communion. Yet not even these other acts could unite you as closely to God as can do this packing, if and when the packing is the duty of certain moments, and if, and as, the little old daughter does this her packing with her heart and intention turned to

God her Home, if she offers her packing as her service, that service which is perfect liberty.

Not even a soul already in Heaven, not even an angel or archangel, can take your place there; for what God wants, what God will love to accept, in those rooms, in those packing days, and from your packing hands, will be just this little packing performed by you in those little rooms. Certainly it has been mainly through my realising this doctrine a little, and through my poor little self-exercising in it, that I have got on a bit, and you will get on faster than I have done with it. You understand? At one moment, packing; at another, silent adoration in Church; at another, dreariness and unwilling drift; at another, the joys of human affections given and received; at another, keen suffering of soul, of mind, in apparent utter loneliness; at another, external acts of religion; at another, death itself. All these occupations every one can, ought, and will be, each when and where, duty, reason, conscience, necessity—God—calls for it; it will all become the means and instruments of loving, of transfiguration, of growth for your soul, and of its beatitude. But it is for God to choose these things, their degrees, combinations, successions; and it is for you just simply, very humbly, very gently and peacefully, to follow that leading.

'Per Crucem ad Lucem.'

SL, pp. 286-287

Certainly it is perseverance in the spiritual life, on and on ... that supremely matters: here the long pull, the 'how to become a Christian when one already is one', the plodding Alpine step is to the fore in his counselling of moderation and of the avoidance of strain in the religious life.

To G. G.   (*October 6, 1919*)

I want to write now, also, because, since you cannot come just now (very naturally, though I am truly sorry), I should like to make some remarks upon quite a number of practical points or questions raised by you since last I wrote.

I. As to the practical points.

1. Much frequentation of the Cathedral. [G. G. was now living in Salisbury.] You know well, how greatly I love this for you. Yet there is one warning I would give you, and would beg you to bear in mind. *Do not overdo it*; I mean, do not take your utter fill, while the attraction is thus strong. If we want our fervour

to last, we must practise moderation even in our prayer, even in our Quiet. And certainly it is perseverance in the spiritual life, on and on, across the years and the changes of our moods and trials, health and environment: it is this that supremely matters. And you will add greatly to the probabilities of such perseverance, if you will get into the way (after having settled upon the amount of time that will be wise for you to give to the Cathedral, or your prayer of quiet in general) of keeping a little even beyond this time, when you are dry; and a little short of this time, when you are in consolation. You see why, don't you? Already the Stoics had the grand double rule: *abstine et sustine*: 'abstain and sustain': i.e., moderate thyself in things attractive and consoling; persevere, hold out, in things repulsive and desolating. There is nothing God loves better, or rewards more richly, than such double self-conquest as this! Whereas all those who heedlessly take their glut of pleasant things, however sacred these things may be, are in grave danger of soon outliving their fervour, even if they do not become permanently disgusted.

SL, p. 290

The Huvelin sayings referred to were some he had copied from his old spiritual master and the guide of so many in his generation. Ten of them are included in the counsels that follow these letters.

To G. G.   (*January 2, 1920*)

I had counted upon writing my first 1920 letter to you; but, alas, strict duty intervened, and forced me to write to other three people instead. But I want you to look upon this scribble as though written on New Year's Day itself.

I want, then, to wish you a very rich, deep, true, straight and simple growth in the love of God, accepted and willed gently but greatly, *at the daily, hourly cost of self*. I have to try my little old best more than ever at this, now; for I find that any and all brooding or sulking or useless self-occupation—any pride or vanity at once disturbs or dries up my incubation-work. Professor James Ward and I agreed one day, that nothing in philosophy, still more in religion, should ever be attempted in and with the first clearness (what, e.g., journalists are content with, and have to be content with), but in and with the *second clearness*, which only comes after that first cheery clarity has gone, and has been succeeded by a dreary confusion and obtuseness of mind. Only this second clearness, rising up like something in no wise one's own, from the depths of one's sub-conscious-ness—only this is any good in such great matters. And this pro-cess is costly, humiliating, and very easily disturbed by rubbishy self-occupations.

I am so glad you are trying to work the *Imitation* into your life; it is the only way to read it which is really worthy of what itself is so intensely alive. Now *there* is a book written as should be all religious books; they should be the quintessence of a long experience and fight in suffering and self-transformation. Also the 20 Huvelin sayings—they sprang straight from a life pene-trated by God and the deepest love of Him. I will, a little on, copy out for you another 20 sayings—they are all, please God, at work within me; and how happy, if they can get to work in my niece child also!

As to my *Apocalyptic Element*, keep it as long as you feel re-reading it can help you. I have two or three other papers which may also be of use to you. But, you see, with religious reading I always feel the situation is different from more ordinary read-ing. I mean, that religious reading should always be select, slow, ruminating, and given to comparatively few books or papers. So we will, when you are again ready, get on with our Greek things—plenty of *them*—and, alongside, and behind them all, will be our few deepest readings, full of prayer, full of self-humiliation, full of gentle attempts, gently to will whatever suffering God may *kindly* send us. A Jesuit novice once told me, with kindling countenance, how grand he found the practice of *at once* meeting suffering with joy. God alone can help us succeed in this; but what is Christianity, if it be not something like that?

SL, pp. 298–299

To G. G.   (*March 5, 1920*)

I am sure that when say, 20 years hence, you look back upon your life, you will specially thank God for this double current I have tried to establish in your mind and soul: the current directly religious—this very pure in quality and genially costly; the current not directly religious, this also very large and deep—a great bucket of pure water into which to drop drops of the purest religious wine. This greatly helps us to escape all reactions. . . .

SL, p. 300

The way to face the inevitable times of aridity and dryness are tellingly described by an old veteran who has also had the good fortune to have known sound counselors in the course of his journey.

To G. G.   *(April 21, 1920)*

Let me give you three images, all of which have helped me on along 'many a flinty furlong'. At eighteen I learnt from Father Raymond Hocking, that grandly interior-minded Dominican, that I certainly could, with God's grace, give myself to Him, and strive to live my life long with Him and for Him. But that this would mean winning and practising much desolation—that I would be climbing a mountain where, off and on, I might be enveloped in mist for days on end, unable to see a foot before me. Had I noticed how mountaineers climb mountains? how they have a quiet, regular, short step—on the level it looks petty; but then this step they keep up, on and on, as they ascend, whilst the inexperienced townsman hurried along, and soon has to stop, dead beat with the climb. Such an expert mountaineer, when the thick mists come, halts and camps out under some slight cover brought with him, quietly smoking his pipe, and moves on only when the mist has cleared away.

Then in my thirties I utilised another image, learnt in my Jesuit Retreats. How I was taking a long journey on board ship, with great storms pretty sure ahead of me; and how I must now select, and fix in my little cabin, some few but entirely appropriate things—a small trunk fixed up at one end, a chair that would keep its position, tumbler and glass that would do ditto: all this, simple, strong, and selected throughout in view of stormy weather. So would my spirituality have to be chosen and cultivated especially in view of 'dirty' weather.

And lastly, in my forties another image helped me—they all three are in pretty frequent use still! I am travelling on a camel across a huge desert. Windless days occur, and then all is well. But hurricanes of wind will come, unforeseen, tremendous. What to do then? It is very simple, but it takes much practice to do well at all. Dismount from the camel, fall prostrate face downwards on the sand, covering your head with your cloak. And lie thus, an hour, three hours, half a day: the sandstorm will go, and you will arise, and continue your journey as if nothing had happened. The old Uncle has had many, many such sandstorms. How immensely useful they are!

You see, whether it be great cloud-mists on the mountain-side, or huge, mountain-high waves on the ocean, or blinding sand-storms in the desert : there is each time one crucial point—to form no conclusions, to take no decisions, to change nothing during such crises, and especially at such times, not to force any particularly religious mood or idea in oneself. To turn gently to other things, to maintain a vague, general attitude of resignation —to be very meek, with oneself and with others : the crisis goes by, thus, with great fruit. What is a religion worth which costs you nothing? What is a sense of God worth which would be at your disposal, capable of being comfortably elicited when and where you please? It is far, far more God who must hold us, than we who must hold Him. And we get trained in these dark-nesses into that sense of our importance without which the very presence of God becomes a snare.

As to your feeling the facts of life and of religion complicated —*that* would be, I expect, in any oppressive way, only during such desolations. Yet I want to note this point for you—viz. that though I believe your *Confessions* and *Imitation* (with Psalms and New Testament), and the Church Service, do not strain you, nor, I think, my letters written specially for yourself, I am not at all sure of my writings in this respect. I mean that they are the writings of, I believe, a masculine mind—that they contain far more sheer thinking that is suited to a woman—even a woman with as rarely much intellect as yourself, Child. This is why I was slow to give or to lend you my writings. Yet I did so, because I want you to feel that there is also much hard thinking, much unpettifying of the great lesson which God's world and work convey if we can and do front them fairly. I wanted you, even in times of temptation, to feel the realities you were called to, perhaps straining at times—even apparently mere illusions—but not cramping, not petty. You can thus settle quietly into your little cabin with the huge billows buffeting you, the ship : their size has not been minimised : they *are* huge : well, God is in the storm as in the calm! But, of course, I am deeply glad the sunshine and calm are back again. And certainly these, and these at their utmost, are intended for our eventual life!

> Par passage pénible
> Passons à port plaisant,

carved a prisoner on the wall of his cell, during his long im-prisonment in the White Tower of the Tower of London. *That*

is just it; both are true, both are facts : the *pénible* of the *passage,*
and the *plaisant*—oh, its grand expanse—of the *port.*

SL, pp. 304–306

To G. G.   (*May, 4, 1920*)

And your and my work is *just the same,* if we learn to do it
simply for God, simply as, here and now, the *one* means of
growing in love for Him. To-day it is cooking, scrubbing; to-
morrow it may be utterly different : death itself will come in
due time, but, before it, still many a joy and many a training.
We will gently practise a genial concentration upon just the one
thing picked out for us by God. *How* this helps! *How* greatly we
add to our crosses by being cross with them! More than half our
life goes in wishing for things other than those sent us. Yet it is
these things, as sent, and when willed and at last loved as sent,
that train us for Home, that can form a spiritual Home for us
even here and now.

The Fioretti's chapters are each complete in itself. Five minutes would give you rich food. And didn't St. Francis know such
troubles as yours,—bigger than yours, and didn't he just rise to
them in all-transforming love!

To-morrow I am 68, yet, thank God, I feel fresh and young in
soul. . . .

SL, p. 306

To G. G.   (*June 23, 1920*)

The wise way to fight antipathies is *never* to fight them
directly—turn gently to other sights, images, thoughts, etc. If
it—the hate—persists, bear it gently like a fever or a toothache—
do not speak to it—better not speak of it even to God; but gently
turn to Him your love and life, and tell Him gently that you
want Him and all of Him; and that you beg for courage whilst
He thus leaves you dressed, or seeing yourself dressed in what
you do not want to endorse as a will-decision, but only as purgation if so He wills. It is an itch—scratching makes it worse.
Away out into God's great world, Sweet,—even if your immediate landscape is just your unlovely antipathies.

SL, pp. 306–307

To G. G.   (*August 31, 1920*)

I am struck, too, at a peculiarity here which I have noticed
hundreds of times in actual life and in history. It is how the

little regarded, the very simple, the unbrilliant souls—souls treated by impatient others as more or less wanting—are exactly, pretty often, specially enlightened by God and specially near to Him. And *there*, no doubt, is the secret of this striking interconnection between an apparent minimum of earthly gifts and a maximum of heavenly light. The cause is not that gifts of quick-wittedness, etc., are bad, or are directly obstacles to Grace. No. No. But that quite ordinary intelligence—real slowness of mind—will quite well do as reflections of God's light, and that such limitations are more easily accompanied by simplicity, naiveness, recollection, absence of self-occupation, which dispositions are necessary for the soul's union with God. Such souls more easily approach action—and more easily escape activity. So it was markedly with the Curé d'Ars, a soul you must get to love with me. Yet a man who knew him well told me the Curé had been still simpler than the charming life and notes taken of his sayings make him appear.

A wonderful thoughtful friend insisted to me that the soul's health and happiness depended upon a maximum of *Zest* and as little as possible of *excitement*. *Zest* is the pleasure which comes from thoughts, occupations, etc., that fit into, that are continuous applications, etc., of extant habits and interests of a good kind—duties and joys that steady us and give us balance and centrality. *Excitement* is the pleasure which comes from breaking loose, from fragmentariness, from losing our balance and centrality. Zest is natural warmth—excitement is fever heat. For Zest—to be relished requires much self-discipline and recollection—much spaciousness of mind: whereas the more distracted we are, the more racketed and impulse-led, the more we thirst for excitement, and the more its *sciròcco* air dries up our spiritual sap and makes us long for more excitement.

Feed upon zest—and zest-bringing things—you will more and more become so central that, even if you live thirty years more than this old scribbler, you will be able with little or no human encouragement to escape excitement, lopsidedness, oddity, etc.

SL, pp. 308–309

To G. G.   (*October 26, 1920*)

No doubt a Retreat depends somewhat on the giver of it; yet it really depends far more upon the simplicity and generosity of the soul that makes the Retreat. I am sure you already know well that you must evade all straining, all vehemence, all as it were putting your nerves into it. On the contrary the attention wanted is leisurely expansion—a dropping gently of distractions, of obsessions, etc.—'La fine pointe de l'esprit'. That is the instrument of progress, the recipient of graces. This old scribbler, how much of that dropping, evading—gently waiting—as against his interior vehemences and uproar, a sterile and sterilising restlessness—he has to practise. Yet practice shows him plainly that *that* is what good sense and God want of him. Peace and power come that way and only that way.

I know too that you should never strain, never directly strive to like people. Just merely drop or ignore your antipathies. There again I have been having hurricanes of antipathies—well—to keep quietly ignoring all that rumpus—that is all that God asks, and we then grow through, and on occasion of, these involuntary vehemences. They keep us humble and watchful and close to God. I am so glad you begin your Retreat on All Saints—my favourite Feast—the Feast not only of all the heroic lovers of God that have ever lived—but the Feast of single heroic supernatural acts—even if and where they remained single. May that darling glow, that genial sunshine of the Saints, with Christ their King in their midst, deepen, widen, sweeten, expand, steady this darling little child.

SL, p. 314

To G. G.   *(January 29 and February 2, 1921)*

I guess my Sweet has a time of dryness, of darkness, on. Well, these are times of great fruitfulness, provided we will be patient, force nothing, change no regulation, decide nothing capable of being put off, but gently busy ourselves with such other things as your Greek, etc.

SL, p. 325

To G. G.

I take it that God in His goodness has granted you the simple Prayer of Quiet—or, at least, that you get given touches, short dawns, of it, now and then. You know, dear, how much and often I insist with you on the visible, the historical, the social, the institutional. But this is done without even the temptation to doubt, or to treat lightly, moments of formless prayer. Such formless prayer, where genuine, is, on the contrary, a deep grace, a darling force and still joy for the soul. May you have,

and keep, and grow in this grace! What are the tests, the conditions of this genuineness? They are two. Such prayer may
never become the soul's only form of prayer; formal, vocal or
mental prayer—the reciting of e.g. the Our Father, the Glory be
to the Father, Acts of Faith, Hope, Love, Contrition (as in the
prayer-books or made up by oneself)—prayers, all these, we can
give an account of when we have done them : such prayers must
never cease. And such formless prayer is the right sort if, in
coming away from it, you find yourself humbler, sweeter, more
patient, more ready to suffer, more loving (in effect even more
than in affection) towards God and man; given the first (precaution) and this second (result) you cannot well have too much
of this prayer. And I think God will lead you much along this
path; and that you will get beyond the worldliness, and other
faults, especially through it. For you will get to love it so; and it
will grow or will intermit, in proportion as you are faithful in
turning away from self. A homely heroism will feed this prayer
of speechless love; and the speechless love will feed the homely
heroism.

   LTN, pp. 43-44

   Again the counsel on suffering as the potentially holiest form of
action probes to the core of his spiritual wisdom.

To G. G.   *(October 7, 1921)*

   You bring up, my Child, a point which I suppose you really
feel an objection. Even if you do not feel it so, I think it well
worth while to clear out this corner of your mind, so as to make
quite sure that you correctly seize the truly great doctrine of
Purgatory. I want, then, to make sure that you clearly understand that, according to that doctrine, suffering (*rightly accepted
suffering*) is indeed usually necessary for, is inherent in, the
Purification from sin, evil habits, etc. But it makes no substantial
distinction between such Purification as taking place already
here, or taking place in the Beyond. In all our Retreats we are
taught that it will have been our own fault, if the sufferings of
our life here have not sufficed to purify us from our sins and
evil habits. Of course, even very great sufferings would not,
simply of themselves, purify us from even small evil habits. It
is only suffering *meekly accepted, willed, transfigured by love
of God, of Christ*—it is only such, that will purify or cure anything. This is so true that, where the love is perfect, this *love*

alone, without any suffering not directly prompted by itself, completely blots out the evil dispositions. Such a soul, even if previously a great sinner, goes straight to Heaven upon its death. Yet, in all cases, Purgatory applies indifferently to suffering rightly borne in *this* life and the same similarly borne in *that* life. There is simply no such thing, as a Purgatory hereafter. On the contrary, every pang God allows to reach us here, and which we manage to bear a little well, does *a work not to be repeated.* We become thus fitter and fitter for complete union with Christ and God from the very minute of our death.

I have written 'a little well' on purpose. For to suffer well is far more difficult than to act well (although the ordinary talk is that we have just 'to grin and bear' suffering—we can do nothing to it or with it ! ! !). Holy suffering is the very crown of holy action. And God is no pedant : He can and does look to the substance of our suffering, and knows how to penetrate beyond our surface restlessness or murmurs. Indeed, part of the great work suffering effects in the soul doubtless springs from the way in which, when acute, it almost invariably humbles us : we can much less easily cut a fine figure in our own eyes over our sufferings, than we can over our actions when in peace and plenty.

You understand all the above completely, I trust? We will both do what gently, peaceably we can to have all our Purgatory—every drop of it—here; and then Heaven, the closest union, unfailing, with Pure Joy, with All Purity, with Christ, with God.

SL, p. 340

'To a Lady', as Bernard Holland designates this letter, is in fact to Mrs Stuart Moore (Evelyn Underhill) and reveals what was referred to in the introductory chapter as his highly discriminating effort to get established at least a minimal basis for her accepting the historical fact of the Christian faith.

To a Lady   *(December 26–29, 1921)*

I should like a certain DEFINITE TIME GIVEN each day to DELIBERATE PRAYER, which would not be much added to in times of consolation, nor much detracted from in times of desolation. But such fixed time for prayer—as over and above your Church doings—should not be long. What you propose in your time-table will do very well indeed. Of course, we are talking simply of deliberate prayer—whatever kind and degree of this suits you best—i.e., most strengthens you to love, to work and to suffer, and most humbles yet braces you. For as to the spirit of prayer, inarticulate prayer, the prayerful disposition: this should more and more penetrate all your walking hours.

You tell me that you could not truthfully profess belief in certain supposed Historical Facts. I suppose these to be the Virgin Birth, the Bodily Resurrection, the Johannine Miracles at least primarily. But pray note that, even so, *you can still retain the more general, and the bed-rock principle of the Catholic mind.* I should feel that you were not clear as to your own deepest instincts or were being unfaithful to them, if you could not, or did not, humbly set about full, definite development of the principle I have in view. Now and then it shows in your acts, temper of mind; and then it disappears for a while, overlain by thoughts or moods of another, a quite contrary, provenance. Let us work, gently but wholeheartedly, at getting this principle to become one of the chief beams in your spiritual edifice, *part of the rock,* known and willed at all times, *of your Faith.*

There are, then, two possible positions with regard to Historical Happenings (two positions, I mean, over and above the ordinary orthodox position that the Church not only holds a list of Spiritual Truths, but knows which of these Spiritual Truths is also a Factual Happening, and that this its knowledge is infallible, unchanging, and binding upon all men to the end of time. I am not asking this of you). You can hold that Historical Happenings *generally,* that *some* Historical Happenings, are necessary; that belief in them is necessary, to every at all powerful and perfect religion, hence especially so to Christianity. Or you can hold that Historical Happenings even quite *generally,* that *no* Historical Happening, that *no* belief in any Historical Happening, is ever an essential part of religion; that religion generally, and Christianity in particular, can flourish—will flourish, after every single supposed Historical Fact has been demonstrated non-historical, and after all men have come to recognise this complete *defactualising* of religion.

How I am very sure that the position which holds that *some* Historical Happenings, that the non-refutedness of their historical character, and that definite belief in this genuine Historicalness, are *essential ingredients of every powerful and at all perfect religion*—especially Christianity—is true. And I am quite sure that the opposite position—the reduction of religion to a system of mere ideas—principles, etc.—is *profoundly* false. But when

then, I come to watch your mind and soul, I find certain vol-
canic eruptions in favour of position No. 1; yet also whole tracts
of intervening, as it were slowly accumulated aqueous formations, which really imply, or even spring from, position No. 2.
If you could, and would gradually, but most thoroughly, drop
and eliminate all the position No. 2, you would be left (even
without adding any one item to the list of Historical Happenings
held by yourself to be such) with an outlook possessing the fundamental Catholic quality.

I note that you do not 'at present understand in the least the
religious feeling of the need of a half-way house between one's
self and God'. I note, too, that 'the human-historical values'
appear to you as of secondary importance. Now here I cannot
help feeling a serious weakness and *lacuna*, indeed an incon-
sistency, in your psychology, your analysis of the religious
temper, and in your own, at least implied, attitude on other
occasions. As you probably know as well as I do, all the finest
recent psychology, indeed also the deepest epistemology, show
us, and insist upon, how we, poor human beings, at least in this
life, never begin (or in the long run keep up) the apprehension
of things spiritual except on occasion of the awakedness and
stimulation of the senses. That is, there is no such thing as an
exclusively spiritual awakening to, or apprehension of, spiritual
Realities. This, to my mind, is already decisive against all purely
spiritual, entirely mystical, quite non-historical, quite non-
successive religion.

Next, religiously, the human soul, upon the whole, in the
long run, in its richest developments, certainly, I think, requires
not a half-way house for it on its way to God, but *God Himself
to come down to it*, not half-way but *the whole way*. To put it
in the most homely way : surely the infant does not feel its
mother's breast a 'half-way house', a queer artificial *intermezzo*
between itself and its mother; but the infant feels that breast as
the self-giving of that mother, as a self-compression, a touching
condescension for bringing the mother's own life to the infant,
and thus gradually to raise this infant to the mother's strength
and stature. St. Augustine surely, surely, had got this point right,
in spite of the great attractions which, quite certainly, a purely
spiritual religion possessed for wide stretches of his mind. He
felt that it was this condescension, *this coming down to us of
God*, His appearing to us in human form and ways, which
'nourished love and ousted inflation'. Quite, quite right! *That*

alone, at least in some form and degree, will ever give us a religion sufficiently lowly, homely, humbling. . . .

God does dwell in, and manifests Himself by, Historical Happenings—here, more than there; now, more than then. But this spells grades of Divine Self-Revelation. And, since in the higher and highest reaches of spiritual reality the differences of degree issue more and more in differences of kind, we reach at least an apex of spirituality which is, at bottom, the deepest, fullest self-abasement of God—Jesus Christ, in the Manger, on the Cross. . . .

P.S. I much like your love for your cats. I deeply love my little dog; and Abbé Huvelin was devoted to his cat. We all three can and will become all the dearer to God for this our love of our little relations, the smaller creatures of God. Again it was God incarnate, it was Jesus of Nazareth, of Gethsemane, of Calvary, and not pure Theism, that first taught this.

SL, pp. 348-350

Von Hügel's readiness to use any incident out of his own life that he thought could help another is well illustrated in this letter to a young girl.

To a Girl (*on her Confirmation, Anglican*)   (*April 11, 1922*)

I know that you are to be confirmed to-morrow, and I feel an inward pressure to write you a little letter on this important step in your life. If you were engaged to be married, I would certainly write to you; so why should I not about an act, different indeed, but not necessarily less important?

Let me then go back in my mind to when I was your own age, and try to get on to paper one predominant desire which then came into my own inner life. You see, when I began to try to be good—to serve God—I already, alas, found myself involved in gravely bad habits and inclinations. But this, once I was, by God's grace, awakened to long to be straight and true—to go direct to God and Christ—had one great advantage. I saw young fellows all round me fretting to be *free*, to be their own sole, full masters. They fretted against this and that thing; against this and that person. They thought if only they could get away from these, they would be free. But I myself *could not feel that to be nearly enough;* I was too little happy in myself to fiddle-faddle at such little things! I wanted, *I had to*, get rid of—not those outside conditions, not those other people and their orders, etc.: but I had, somehow, to become free from *self*, from my poor, shabby, bad, all-spoiling *self*! *There* lay freedom, *there* lay happiness! And I see now at 70, more clearly again than at 17, that I was right there. That all external things, all persons, even if and when they may be not to our natural liking, that they none can really hurt us,—indeed, that they all of them can readily help us, once we are awake, spiritually awake; and that our service of God really means for us the fighting of self. Of course God's service includes also our service of others—our relations, our friends. And again, even the whole of religion is not the whole of our activities and interests—is *rightly* not the whole. Yet it remains most true that our religion begins to be our romance—our most solid, sustaining romance—only on the day on which it becomes adult and quite real—that is, only on the day on which we wake up to self and determine to fight it.

Do not think, my dear, that I am comparing you with myself as I was then. No, whatever may be your faults, you are a far better girl than I was a boy. Not that I am thinking of any particular faults of yours. I do not know you well enough to be able to do *that*. I am only facing the two quite general, but quite sufficiently rousing facts: that we all of us have 'selves' (the enemies of our true, good selves) to fight, and that only so fighting are we adult, fruitful and happy.

SL, pp. 351–352

Mrs Lillie was an American admirer of von Hügel's who had printed in a private edition a group of the letters which the Baron had written to her. The figure of science as a coral-reef built up from below and of religion as a golden shower from above is one of his happiest and is a fitting one with which to close this selection of the letters of counsel.

To Mrs Lillie   *(April 20, 1922)*

It seems to me that, from sheer enthusiasm, you become unconsciously unfair both to Science and to Religion. Unfair to Science, because if Science and Religion really produce interchangeable results, and you, notwithstanding, remain definitely religious, you will have, after all, to ask the Scientists more than as such, they give,—indeed, I am sure, more than as such, they *can* give. For all Science, and in the term I include history, psychology, etc., is essentially the ceaseless seeking, the ceaseless restating, the ceaseless discovering of error, and the substituting of something nearer to the truth. I do not see how

Science can be asked to start with a definite God, with a definite
Future Life, with anything like a Church; I think it cannot even
end with anything more than a vague reverence and sense of a
deep background—a very elementary Theism will, at best, and
can hardly, be reached by it: such Theism will be, I believe, its
maximum. Now, Religion, on the contrary, begins with a full
affirmation of a Reality, of a Reality other and more than all
mankind. It is certain of God, certain of Christ, certain of the
Church. It is a gift from above downwards, not a groping from
below upwards. It is not like Science a coral-reef, it is more like
a golden shower from above. Assimilate Religion to Science, and
you have levelled down to something which, though excellent
for Science, has taken from Religion its entire force and good;
(you have shorn Samson of his locks with a vengeance). On the
other hand, force Science up to the level of Religion, or think
that you have done so, and Science affirms far more than, as
such, it can affirm, and you, on your part, are in a world of
unreality. Let me illustrate this by the very example you give
me of the death of Metchnikoff. His final words—'Do not fear
for me, I am not afraid; I have had a Divine light: Science will
solve the problems, the wonderful problems of existence' ... —I
contrast with these Littre's last months with his sense of awe, the
feeling of whole new worlds coming upon him, worlds not of
scientific discovery at all, but the worlds of contrition, of a
sense of sin, of a sense of an immense over-againstness, of a huge
Other before which he felt crushed and a nothing. In the former
case we have the courage, the selflessness, the optimism, of a
true scientist; in the latter we have the elementary religious
instincts. The two things are quite uninterchangeable: my dear
Mrs. Lillie, pray look out to keep, or to gain, the sense of this
difference. May I, though it is a sacred memory to me, just refer
to the death of my eldest daughter in Rome? She was no scientist,
but a Christian, and Catholic believer: she died loving God, with
a sense of God, with an abandonment of herself into God's
Hands, with a love of Christ as God with us, with a hope, with
a trust, to be eternally with Them. Now, of course, I do not
quote this as anything but what occurs again and again among
definitely religious souls, I only quote it to bring out, if I can,
the difference, which—very certainly is there, between the state
of soul of the scientist simply as such, and the state of the
definite religionist. Of course, the complete thing would be to have
both, and certainly both have occurred again and again in the

same soul. There was, for instance, Lord Rayleigh, a great mathematician, a great physicist, who died not long ago, a devout High Anglican who had never missed daily Church since his early manhood.

It was sitting by the side of Abbé Huvelin that I, more vividly than ever before, realised the difference between these two levels, realised their respective necessity, their respective liberty. A splendid Greek scholar, as fine and free as is your Professor as a biologist, and with a fear and horror of the interference of theologians, this sane man was absorbed in the love and service of God, and of his neighbours for the sake of God. For myself I must have both movements: the palace of my soul must have somehow two lifts—a lift which is always going up from below, and a lift which is always going down from above. I must both be seeking and be having. I must both move and repose.—But it is as well that I should stop now: the thing is not merely to see these things but to practise them: to *be* is a very different affair.

With kindest regards from us all three, and with cordial respects to the Professor,

Yours very sincerely,

SL. pp. 353–354   F. von Hügel.

PART TWO

SPIRITUAL COUNSEL FROM THE WORKS OF BARON FRIEDRICH VON HÜGEL

Chapter IV

THE LIFE OF PRAYER

THE rich harvest of spiritual counsel which Baron von Hügel had to give was not confined to his letters but, as has been previously suggested, is sprinkled throughout his profound works on the philosophy of religion and may even be seen to set the frame and purpose of these writings. He is ever so frank about this matter of existential communication and wrote in the introduction to his *Mystical Element of Religion.*

> Kierkegaard used to claim that he ever wrote *existentially*, pricked on by the exigencies of actual life, to attempt their expression in terms of that life, and in view of its further spiritual development. More than ever the spiritual life appears now as supremely worth the having, and yet it seems to raise, or to find, the most formidable difficulties or even deadlocks. I can but hope that these pages may have so largely sprung from the exigencies of that life itself,— that they may have caught so much of the spirit of the chief livers of that spiritual life, especially of St. Catherine of Genoa and of St. John of the Cross, and, above all, of the One Master and Measure of Christianity and of the Church,—as to stimulate such life, its practice, love, and study, in their readers, and may point them, spur them on, through and beyond all that has been attempted, missed or obscured, to fuller religious insight, force and fruitfulness.
> (*ME 1*, p. xxxiii).

The same note marks his preface to *Eternal Life* which concludes with this line, 'There is some reason to hope that these pages may, in turn, live for a while and that they may, here and there, help some religious students and strugglers.' (*EL*, p. vi). He wrote of *Eternal Life* in sending a copy to his niece, 'I wrote the thing praying. Read it as written, child' (*LTN*, p. 72).

This chapter will consist of two remarkable lectures on prayer which are quoted here in their entirety. They were given to a group

of Anglicans at Beaconsfield on October 26th and 27th, 1921 and were
published in a little book called *The Life of Prayer* as well as in the
second series of *Essays and Addresses* issued posthumously in 1926.
There is something highly significant in the order in which these two
lectures were given. It is to be noted that *The Facts and Truths Concerning God* comes first. For von Hügel one dare not talk about
prayer without first talking about the ground of prayer, about God.
For him, prayer is always a response to the Divine initiative. The
prevenient One calls out our prayer, or we should never make it.
Only when this has been firmly established does he move to the
second lecture in which the diagnosis is made of the man who prays.

Neither in these lectures nor in the many passages quoted in the
following chapter does von Hügel give more than hints in the matter
of how prayer is to be practised. His responsibility is taken to be that
of helping to create a climate for the practice of prayer, a climate that
will make the practice of prayer both plausible and congenial. The rest
can alone be given in the highly experimental and private guidance
of personal consultation.

THE FACTS AND TRUTHS CONCERNING GOD AND THE SOUL
WHICH ARE OF MOST IMPORTANCE IN THE LIFE OF PRAYER

I

*The Facts and Doctrines Concerning God which are
of Especial Importance in the Life of Prayer*

I find it impossible to restrict myself here to explicit tests of
Scripture or to the Dogmatic Definitions of the Christian Faith.
On the other hand, I will only put forward certain positions
which have behind them large affirmations or assured implications of Scripture and great Fathers and theologians of the
Church—positions which, if in recent centuries or in our own
times, largely ignored or explained away, nevertheless express
the never extinct Christian and Catholic experience. Working
within these lines and drawing also upon my own fifty years of
endeavor in these matters, I find the positions concerning God,
which require full and intelligent adoption in our life of Prayer
to be seven.

I

God is a stupendously rich Reality—the alone boundlessly rich
Reality. His outward action throughout the Universe—His

creation, sustentation and direction of the world at large—is immensely rich. Still deeper and more delicate is this richness and reality in God's Incarnation and Redemptive Action. Yet His Being, His interior Life, are in no wise exhausted by all this outward Action, nor does this action occasion or articulate His character. We indeed, we little mortals—they too, the greatest of angels—we become our true selves, we articulate our spiritual characters, by apprehending, willing and serving God. But God is God, already apart from His occupation with us. These are the great facts which I believe to be specially revealed to us in the dogma of the Holy Trinity—facts of which we have an especial need in these our times. The whole of the Negative Theology, where it is sound and not really agnostic or pantheistic, is but an attempt to utter vividly this stupendous richness of God.

Our prayer will lack the deepest awe and widest expansion, if we do not find room within it for this fact concerning God. We will thus retain a strong sense that not even Jesus Christ and His Redemption exhaust God. Christian prayer, indeed Christian theology, are thus not Soteriology, practical or theoretical. Here Fénelon's great letters to the Carmelite nun, Soeur Charlotte de S. Cyprien, are admirable in their tender devotion to Christ free from all excessive Christocentrism.

2

God is the author of, and God is variously reflected in, all (innocent) Nature as well as in all Supernature. Here is the doctrine which was central in the outlook of Aquinas and Dante, of St. Francis and of Giotto. It was very largely forgotten or denied afterwards, during the later Middle Ages. And, although the Renaissance and then the Protestant Reformation were (variously wise and wild) protests against the abuses of the later Middle Ages, these movements were themselves largely infected by the impoverished philosophy and the thin theology of these same later Middle Ages. The signs are multiplying that man will return, with such improvements as may be wisely desirable, to that wonderfully rich outlook of the Golden Middle Age, where God's outward action moves on two levels—the natural level and the supernatural level—a Good and a Better or Best—two *kinds,* and not merely two degrees, of Goodness. *We thus recognize in man's actual life a polarity, a tension, a friction, a one thing at work in distinctly another thing*—like yeast in meal, like salt in meat, like coral insects and whole coral reefs in the huge ocean—an ocean so different from themselves. We thus also acquire an explanation, and one which is not discouraging, of the fact that it is a difficult art to prevent religion from over-straining us and from thus leading to a very dangerous reaction against itself. For thus we see that the Beatitude of Heaven—the Direct Vision of God, that the sincere forgiveness of our enemies, the love of them, and that the eager acceptance of suffering, are graces and dispositions beyond, and different from, God apprehended as the dim background or groundwork of our lives, and from the honesties and decencies of average domestic and political life. Such honesties and decencies are also good, and they are necessary for us all, in various degrees and forms; and this, also, as the occasions and material for the supernatural to utilise and transform—the Mountain and the Plain, the Edelweiss, and Alpenrose, and the cornfields and potatoes; here all appear, and this in fruitful contrast and congenital inter-aid.

Such an inclusive and yet discriminating position brings also much help to our prayer. For in prayer, also, it brings a tension, to the verge of strain; and a *détente*, to the verge of relaxation. In both these movements of the soul God can, and God should, be envisaged—in the *détente*, the God of nature, the source of all that is wholesome and homely; and in the tension, the God of supernature, the source of all that is ardent and heroic. We thus escape dullness, monotony and the life—these subtle dangers of the spiritual life.

3

God alone is fully free. Here is another ancient doctrine which calls aloud for resuscitation. It is already clearly formulated by St. Augustine, and Aquinas elaborates it in its fullness. But the later Middle Ages largely lost it, and Protestants to this hour have, in this point, merely extended and hardened the later Mediaeval obtuseness. Indeed, even the present Broad High Churchmen of the type of *Foundations* have, for the most part, elaborated an apologetic with regard to the dread fact of Evil which deliberately eliminates the great doctrine here envisaged. St. Augustine tells us : *'It is already a great freedom to be able*

*not to sin. But the greatest freedom consists in the inability to
sin.'* And Aquinas elaborates how Perfect Freedom consists in
the spontaneous and joyous self-expression of a perfect nature.
Thus God cannot will, God possesses no inclination to, Evil; and
this absence of choice springs from precisely the perfection of
His Freedom.

The persistent and vivid apprehension of this fact will greatly
help our prayer. For thus only are we adequately humbled before
God, since the difference between God and Man is thus, essentially, not a difference, however great, in performance but in
nature. Far beyond the range of our actual sinfulness extends
the range of our potential sinfulness—of the imperfection inherent in our human degree and kind of Freedom. Whereas God
is not only not actually sinful at all—He is incapable of sin, incapable of temptation to sin.

But there exists, not only God Pure, but also God Incarnate,
Jesus Christ. Here, again, there is no actual sinfulness, and here
also the sinlessness is a most wholesome occasion of humility
to ourselves, the manifoldly sinful. In Jesus Christ the closeness
of the union of His human nature with the Divine nature—
with a Divine Person—renders actual sin impossible even in that
Human nature. Nevertheless this human nature in itself is, even
here, not above real temptation. 'He was in all points tempted as
we are, yet without sin,' says the Epistle to the Hebrews (iv. 15).
Here, again, it is important for us to understand that even ·such
temptation—temptation without sin—is an imperfection per-
taining to a certain kind of freedom—to the human kind of freedom—and not a necessary condition of all freedom, of freedom
as such. For thus in Prayer we can, we will, look up to, adore
God, the Perfect Freedom, which contrasts so grandly with our
own poor little freedom—even with our freedom where this
exists in us, and is used by us, at its very best.

4

God is the Supreme Good—of the stone and of the plant, of
the animal, of man, of the angel, but in what wondrously various
degrees both of self-communication on the part of God, and of
consciousness on the part of the creature, as to this gift from
God, and still more as to the Giver, God Himself! In proportion
to the depth and the breadth of any and every creature's nature,
the creature possesses, or can attain to, the consciousness that

God is its sole ultimate rest, sole pure delight. Religion, as distinct from ethics, flies straight at once to this great ultimate fact, to this unique personalist reality, to God as Beatitude and Beatifier. Thus the religious soul, in proportion to the strength of its religion, always reaches beyond all abstract law, all mere sense of duty and of obligation. St. Augustine is the great doctor of this our divine rest and our divine delight.

Our prayer will be immensely enriched and expanded by a persistent cultivation of this sense of God as our true home. For thus the rivalry between God and creatures for the possession of our hearts will become less and less a struggle between a mysterious obligation and a clear fascination, and more and more a competition between an ocean-wide, all penetrating joy, when our souls come to their true, deep selves, and pleasures feverish, fleeting and shallow, when we allow ourselves heedlessly to be carried along by our superficial selves.

5

God, we have thus already found, is, indeed, not all unlike man. For how, if God were all unlike him, could man apprehend God, and love God, and try 'to be perfect even as our heavenly Father is perfect'? Yet God is also *other than man*. Other, because He, God, is a Reality, an Identity, a Consciousness, distinct from the reality, identity, consciousness of any of His creatures or of the sum-total of them. And God is other, because this His distinct Reality is, by its nature, so much higher and richer, not only in degree but in kind, than is the nature of man or of any other creature. 'Man is made in the image and likeness of God.' Yes, but we must not press this as an exhaustive norm, as though God were simply man writ large—man's better and best instincts and conditions on an immense scale. We shall doubtless be much nearer the facts if we think of God as the living Source and the always previous, always prevenient Realisation, in degrees and ways for us ineffable, of our ideals and ever imperfect achievements—a Realisation which must not be taken directly to contain concretely what our conditions and strivings contain ideally. I am deeply convinced that the truth, and hence the fascination of Religion, as really requires some such emphasis on the *unlikeness* of God, as it requires emphasis upon the likeness. So, for instance, 'God is Love' is a central truth proclaimed by the New Testament and by all the saints of God. And so again, 'God careth for us'—that God is full of sympathy for all His creatures, and for man especially, Jesus Himself never ceases to proclaim and to illustrate. Yet we must beware not to press this further, so as to mean suffering in God. For suffering is an evil, and there exists no evil in God : the religious instinct spontaneously and unchangeably hungers after God as Pure Joy. With St. Bernard, in his classic lament on the death of his darling twin brother Gerard, we will hold that there exists the deepest *compassio*, but no *passio* in God.

Yet our hearts long also (though less strongly, I believe) for downright fellow-suffering, when they suffer and when they are exhorted to suffer well. Such fellow-suffering (deeper than ever we ourselves could suffer, and in One who shares with us the evil of suffering, but without any admixture of the far greater evil of sin) is supplied by the Humanity of Our Lord. The Humanity of Jesus Christ, we have already found, brings temptation as near to God as is compatible with Godhead. And now we find this same Humanity of Jesus brings suffering as near to God as is compatible with the same Godhead. Indeed, the sufferings are so great as to require, for their sustainment by His human nature, the presence and action of the Divine nature, of the Divine Person which has conjoined itself to, and which informs, this human nature.

Our prayer will profit greatly if we thus hold firmly and fervently this double truth : of the *Pure Joy of God* and of the *Deep Suffering of Jesus*. For we will thus neither diminish God to a man of but larger size than we little men are, nor will we dehumanize Jesus by ignoring the immense sufferings, as well as the storm and stress—the temptations—of His earthly life. The definition of the Council of Chalcedon, difficult as it may be to apply it in any great detail, will thus continue to enshrine for us, also as praying souls, an imperishable truth : Jesus Christ is both truly God and truly Man.

6

All we have so far said implies or leads up to the great fact and truth : that *we men need God much more than, and very differently from, the way and degree in which God needs us men*. God is the absolute Cause, the ultimate Reason, the Sole True End and Determiner of our existence, of our persistence, of our nature, of our essential calls and requirements. God is all

these things for man. Man is not one of these things for God.
Man comes to this true self by loving God. God is the very ocean
of Himself—of Love—apart from all creation. Thus the positions
between God and Man, and between Man and God, are entirely
uninterchangeable. Hence the most fundamental need, duty,
honour and happiness of man, is not petition, nor even contrition,
nor again even thanksgiving : these three kinds of prayer which,
indeed, must never disappear out of our spiritual lives; but
adoration. Probably the greatest doctor and the greatest prac-
tiser among souls well known to us in these respects, of such
overwhelmingly adoring prayer, is St. Augustine. Never, in spite
of his tenderly anthropomorphic devotion, does the great
African forget this profound non-equality, this non-interchange-
able relation between God and man. Our prayer will greatly
deepen and widen out, if we also develop such a sense—a sense
which is now continually exposed to the subtle testing and sap-
ping of the pure immanentisms and the sentimental anthropo-
centrisms which fill the air.

7

The Prevenience of God thus appears as the root-fact and the
root-truth of all our previous positions. God not only loves us
more and better than we can ever love ourselves, '*carior est illis*'
—to the Gods—'*home quam sibi,*' already Juvenal told us; but
God loved us before we loved, or could love, Him. God's love of
us rendered possible and actual our love of God. This is emphatically proclaimed by the First Epistle of St. John, and is a
favourite doctrine of St. Bernard. Thus the great Cistercian Abbot
bids his monks rise never so early for their night choir prayer
in coldest mid-winter; they will find God awake, Him the
awakener; they will find Him waiting for them, always anticipating even their earliest watches. How scandalously much is this
great fact forgotten in our days, even by otherwise alert preach-
ers to educated congregations! I had much talk with an
Australian nonconformist minister upon this point, some ten
years ago; and he determined to preach it before such a congregation—a large one in London. He afterwards reported to
me that his discourse had made a great stir, crowds of his hear-
ers flocking into the vestry to declare to him that they never in
their lives had heard such doctrine, and how wonderful and
awakening it was!

Our prayer will certainly gain in depth and aliveness, if we thus continually think of God as the true inspirer of our most original-seeming thoughts and wishes, whensoever these are good and fruitful—as Him who secretly initiated what He openly crowns.

I take these to be the seven great facts and doctrines concerning God—His richness, His double action, natural and supernatural, His perfect Freedom, His delightfulness, His otherness, His adorableness and His prevenience. These seven facts, vividly apprehended, will, even singly and how much more if seen conjointly, each penetrating and calling forth the others, bring much depth and breadth, much variety and elasticity into our prayer. This, however, only if we understand plainly that there is no occasion whatsoever for us to constrain ourselves *positively* on these points. I mean that, though a Christian's prayer will suffer in its Christianity, if it consciously and systematically excludes, still more if it denies, any of these facts, yet no one soul, at any one period of its spiritual life, will feel equally attracted to them all. It will be quite enough—indeed it will be the only wise course—if each particular soul, at any one period of its growth, attends positively, affirmatively, and lovingly to two or three, or even to but one of these facts. Thus not any one soul, but the society of souls, the Church of Christ, will simultaneously apprehend and apply all these facts and truths. The Church's several constituents and organs will supplement each other, and will, collectively, furnish a full perception and a full practice of these great facts of God.

II

The Facts and Truths Concerning the Soul which are of Most Importance in the Life of Prayer

Much in human psychology and epistemology has been rendered more clear during the last thirty years or so, and some very ancient misconceptions have now been finally cleared up. Yet the presentation and the penetration of the processes operative in the life of prayer, which we owe to a St. Augustine, a St. Bernard, a St. Teresa, remain unsurpassed, indeed, on the central points, unapproached to this very hour. I take the points which concern the human mind and spirit, indeed man's complex organism generally, in so far as they come largely into play in the life of prayer, to be again seven. The due allocation and utilisation of the seven psychological facts and laws will, very largely, depend upon the degree to which we have adequately and vividly apprehended the seven great facts and truths concerning God. Indeed, a certain amount of overlapping and repetition is unavoidable as between the two series of facts, where each set of facts is, doubtless, in itself, very distinct from the other set, yet where the one set has to be apprehended by, and has to be put into close relation with, the other set.

I

The decisive preparation for prayer lies not in the prayer itself, but in the life prior to the prayer. That is distractions and dryness, indeed even the real fruitlessness in and of our prayer, spring largely from our faulty dispositions, doings and driftings when out of prayer. The effects of such faultinesses pursue us when we come to pray. The cure for such faults committed out of prayer, and for their effects upon and within prayer, lies in the very wise ordering, and in the very faithful execution of such ordering, of our active life.

Fénelon pointed out to the Duc de Chevreuse how overburdened, and how racketed and distracted was the Duke's life, outside of his direct and deliberate praying; and how greatly that over-burdenedness, when out of prayer, damaged his recollection when in prayer. Fénelon advised the Duke to begin his day with quietly running through in his mind the chief things he would probably have to do, or would probably be solicited to do, during that coming day. That he should then and there reduce the number of such things as much as was wisely possible. And that, when he came to the actual doing of these things, he should clip his action of all unnecessary detail and development. *In this way he would succeed in placing such action within a circumambient air of leisure—of leisure for the spirit of prayer and peace.* This would be like the ordering of a wise gardener, who carefully sees to it that the young trees he plants have sufficient spaces each from the other—have sufficient air in which to grow and expand. I have myself greatly profited by striving to practise this advice.

St. Catherine of Genoa's method of life has also helped me much. She would quietly concentrate, each moment, upon that moment's special content—upon God's gift and will of special suffering or joy, of determination, effort, decision and the like,

conveyed within that moment. Such a scheme follows out something similar, within the spiritual life, to the action of the sun
upon the sun-dial in physical life. The sun successively touches
and illumines this, and then that, and then the next radius of
the dial. Or, again, the scheme reminds one of Goethe's old
mother, Frau Rath, who, when one day an acquaintance, ignor-
ant of Frau Rath's condition, called at her door and asked to see
her, sent down a message to the visitor that 'Frau Rath was busy
dying'. Indeed, a genial, quiet death to self lies in every minute,
when the minute is thus taken separately as the dear will and
the direct vehicle of God.

2

The ceaseless interdependence of Soul and Body. The more
any state of soul—any *psychosis*—is mental, still more is spiritual, or at least the more the agent or patient feels the psychosis
to be thus mental or spiritual, the less, as a rule, is the neural
accompaniment, the neural limitation, and the neural cost of
this state perceived at the time by the experiencing soul. Yet
such accompaniment, limitation and cost are certainly present,
even in the most genuine and highest of man's spiritual actions
or states: indeed, the neural cost appears, roughly, to rise in
proportion as the action, at the time, fails to bring with it any
sense of cost at all.

Fénelon is admirably awake to this important fact, when he
warns Madame de Montberon not to indulge, beyond a certain
limited time, in prayer or quiet—a prayer which greatly helped
and refreshed her; and this because of the neural cost of such
effortless-seeming prayer.

One quite general, yet very helpful preparation towards the
practice of sobriety in prayer, and hence towards escaping, as
far as possible, the acute reactions liable to follow upon such
very delightful prayer, is admirably preached and practised by
Jean Nicholas Grou. This fine classical scholar, and deeply spiritual writer and leader of souls, urges *the importance of the soul's
possession and cultivation of two levels and kinds of action and
interest*—a wholesome natural interest and action, and a deep
supernatural interest and action. The soul will then possess and
will cultivate a genuine interest in politics or economics, in
language or history, in natural science or philosophy—in these,
as part of its bread-winning or as quite freely chosen studies.

And we will thus, when in dryness and even in anticipation of it, possess a most useful range of interest to which to turn, as our disporting ground, in relief of the dreariness or the strain of our directly religious life. I believe Grou's spiritual writings remain so fresh, because (given his spiritual experience) he never, as he tells us himself, wrote on religious subjects except when the spiritual light and fervour were within him; whilst at other— the far more frequent—times he translated Plato or emended the texts of Livy and Horace.

Some further hints towards the bearing and the utilization of desolation, as part and parcel of every at all religious life, and of every at all complete self-knowledge possessed by the liver of such a life. Thus St. Teresa, especially in her Autobiography, gives us admirably vivid descriptions of her times of dryness. On the other hand, I was surprised and disappointed when, some fifteen months ago that deeply sincere Indian convert, the Sadhu Sundar Singh, told me that, never since his conversion thirteen years before, had he ever suffered one moment of spiritual dryness. I believe, with a very experienced psychologist and philosopher friend of mine, that this opinion indicates a strange lack of self-knowledge, perhaps also of what is precisely meant by such dryness, on the part of this devoted Christian. If, then, spiritual dryness is indeed inevitable in the life of prayer, we will be much helped to bear these desert stretches, by persistent recognition—hence also, indeed especially, in our times of fervour—of the normality and the necessity of such desolation. We will thus come to treat desolation in religion as we treat the recurrence of the night within every twenty-four hours of our physical existence; or as bodily weariness at the end of any protracted exertion in our psychic life. When desolation is actually upon us, we will quietly modify, as far as need be, the kind and the amount of our prayer—back, say, from prayer of quiet to ordinary meditation, or to vocal prayer—even to but a few uttered aspirations. And, if the desolation is more acute, we will act somewhat like the Arab caravans behave in the face of a blinding sandstorm in the desert. The men dismount, throw themselves upon their faces in the sand; and there they remain, patient and uncomplaining, till the storm passes, and until, with their wonted patient endurance, they can and do continue on their way.

There are generally a weakness and an error at work within us, at such times, which considerably prolong the trouble, and

largely neutralise the growth this very trouble would otherwise
bring to our souls. The weakness lies in that we let our imagination and sensitiveness be directly absorbed in our trouble. We
contemplate, and further enlarge, the trouble present in ourselves, instead of firmly and faithfully looking away, either at
the great abiding realities of the spiritual world, or, if this is
momentarily impossible for us, at some other, natural or human,
wholesome fact or law. And the error lies in our lurking sus-
picions that, for such trials to purify us, we must feel them fully
in their tryingness—that is, we must face and fathom them
directly and completely. Such a view completely overlooks the
fact that such trials are sent us for the purpose of deoccupying
us with our smaller selves; and, again, it ignores the experience
of God's saints across the ages, that, precisely in proportion as
we can get away from direct occupation with our troubles to the
thought and love of God, to the presence of Him who permits
all this, in the same proportion do and will these trials purify
our souls.

3

The great difference, in spiritual range and depth, in special
attrait and peculiar calls and gifts, *is unchangeably inherent in
each soul's vocation to what it is, and still more to what God would
have it become.* True, certain differences, perceptible on the surface, between soul and soul, largely spring from some change-
able causes or defects. And, again, at the opposite end, the ultimate limitations as well as the possible final calls of individual
souls are completely known to God alone, and to the soul itself,
with some real knowledge, only and when, it has advanced considerably on the spiritual way. Still, even the soul which is but
a beginner can, with a little reflection and some good advice,
save itself either much unnecessary failure, or, again, much
vagueness and superficiality of endeavour, if it sorts out, roughly
and for practical purposes, those acts, habits, intentions, self-
conquests, etc., which specially appeal to it in its deepest, most
peaceful moments, or which are specially called for by its particular character in the peculiar circumstances of its life and call :
if it fixes upon *these* dispositions and virtues, and makes *these*
things the central objects of its prayers and endeavours. It will
work at these things—at least for a while—on a relatively wide
and deep scale, and, as to the other virtues and dispositions, it

will be content with not completely neglecting them. If we are faithful and humble in this concentration and cultivation, we shall come to discover any serious mistakes we may have made in our original choice, and we can then correspondingly widen, or narrow, or shift the field, or alter the methods of our operations.

All this directly concerns our prayer also. For all such choosing of the field of our spiritual self-cultivation, all our labours in this field, all our little successes, many failures, and long awaitings of *some* fruit: all this should be *saturated with prayer*—by the spirit of prayer and by definite prayer, vocal, mental or of quiet. And, again, these several kinds of prayer, or combinations of kinds: these too, of course, should be chosen with due care and circumspection, according, again, to the *attrait*, the need, and the experience of the particular soul, which, however, must never be allowed to eliminate all vocal prayer.

Bishop Creighton wrote a fine letter, given in his *Life*, on the wonderfully rich variety which characterised the spiritual life of the Mediaeval Church at its best; and, indeed, such varieties continue to flourish in the Roman Catholic Church. When Frederick William Faber preached the panegyric of St. Ignatius Loyola, on the occasion of the Feast of the Founder of the Jesuits, in the Jesuit church at Farm Street, he spent an hour in unbroken, sympathetic, indeed fervent, exposition of this saint's spirituality, and only in his last sentence did he introduce the necessary limitation and expansion: 'This, then, my dear brethren, is St. Ignatius's way to heaven; and, thank God, it is not the only way.'

A friend of mine, who loved her garden, told me how only one of the many gardeners employed by her had succeeded with every one of her roses. She asked him what was the secret of his success. He told her that the other gardeners treated all her roses, not unwisely, but too generally—they treated them all in precisely the same way; whereas he himself watched across the months each rose-bush separately, and followed out, for each plant, that plant's special *attrait* as to soil, manure, sun, air, water, support, shelter and the like. So with souls: let us, without undue self-occupation, learn to discriminate between them and, again, between them all and ourselves, so as both to respect and encourage *their* ways, however different from our own, and to persevere and improve in *our* ways, however lonely these ways may be.

4

The Incarnation side of religion may never be despised nor forgotten, but must always be assigned *some* definite place and power within our spiritual lives. The approach to God and the condescension of God, the Invisible, Pure Spirit, on occasion of, in, and with the Sensible and Visible—the Historical, Traditional, Social, Sacramental—must remain and be cultivated within our souls.

The fact is that Pure Mysticism is but Pantheism; and that Pantheism is, on principle and incurably, a non-moral, a supra-moral and a non-personalist position, within which there is really no place for a distinct and definite God, for Sin, for Contrition, for the sense of our being creatures, and for Adoration. All attempts to interpret the whole life and teaching of Jesus, as simply the supreme unfolding of Pure Mysticism, suffer shipwreck against the great convictions which colour all the words and deeds of Jesus, that the consummation is indeed proximate, but not present; that its beginnings can indeed already be seen, but not its fulfilment; and that even these beginnings, and still more the fulfilment, are the deed of God, the immensely Personalist Power, and not the work of mankind, still less just the operation of the world-whole. The supreme revelation of the omnipresent, non-successive God, took place, in unique fashion and degree, in such and such years, and months and days and hours, and in such and such places, of human history. And so, similarly, with His lesser, yet still real, self-communications.

Now there is no doubt that *the prayer of quiet*—that *a certain formless recollection and loving feeding upon the sense and presence of God*—of God, as here and now—is a most legitimate prayer. Indeed, for the souls which possess the call to, and capacity for, such prayer (and their number is, I believe, not so very small), this form of prayer will feed and fortify their spirit more than would, *at the times when such prayer can healthily operate*, any number of vocal prayers, formal meditations, or Church services. Nevertheless—and this is our present special point—such prayer of quiet will remain safe and wholesome only if *some* daily vocal prayers, and *some* more or less frequent Church attendances and sacramental acts and receptions, continue active within this same soul's life. I know well that such sensible and spiritual practices will, to such a soul, bring with them, at least at their beginnings, a feeling of incongruity, of oppression, of contraction, sometimes only dull, but at other times very acute. Yet every such initial discomfort, if only the sensible-spiritual acts be chosen with reasonable reference to this soul's special call, and if these acts be bravely faced and persevered in, will (if not promptly, at least in the long run) be followed by an increase, very real, and mostly also clearly perceived, of the substantiality, and of humble, childlike quality in the prayer of quiet, and in the entire character of this same soul.

Let me illustrate what I mean from my own direct experience. After practising a daily three-point meditation for some twenty-five years, the new Helper sent me by God advised me that my prayer should now be mainly informal—more of the prayer of quiet type; but that there should always remain short vocal prayers morning and night, Mass and Holy Communion twice a week, with Confession once a week or once a fortnight; and (perhaps most characteristic point of all) one decade of the rosary every day—this especially to help prevent my interior life from losing touch with the devotion of the people. After over thirty years of this mixed *régime*, I am profoundly convinced of the penetrating sagacity of this advice.

Let me, then suggest that we should each of us discover, with sufficient detail, what is the form of prayer to which God appears to call us; let us give ample room and opportunity to this particular form; but let us also organise, most carefully, a certain regular amount of the other kinds of prayer and worship.

5

The right attitude towards the Sex-instinct, and as to what is, for the Christian, the sin of sins.

Original Sin was generally considered by Catholic Christians, up to the advent of the great Jesuit theologians, as a *stain*, a vicious habit present within human souls from the moment of their conception and birth into this earthly life. And especially St. Augustine, following and still further accentuating the attitude of St. Paul, found this vicious habit to lie centrally in the vehemence of the sex-instinct. Not even St. Augustine dared censure the sex-instinct as such; as a Catholic Christian, he could not cast a slur upon marriage in its essentials. He declared a moderate, readily controllable sex-instinct to be right; only the vehemence, such as now characterises this instinct, was evil and part of original sin.

But the great Jesuit theologians found even this much to be untenable: how could an instinct, without which men would certainly not face the grave burdens of bringing dependent families into the world, be too strong, if we grant that the perpetuation of the human race really matters? So these Jesuit theologians placed the evil, not in the instinct, nor even in the vehemence of the instinct, but simply in the weakness of the reason and of the will called upon to control and moderate that vehemence.

Certain difficulties attach also to this view. Yet this view is satisfactory in that it removes all grounds for pains of conscience as to the presence of the sex-instinct, however strong this sex-instinct may be (apart, of course, from such strength as it may possess owing to the bad or slack life led by the soul which thus experiences the instinct).

Now I believe it to be of great importance that we should realise, vividly and persistently, that human purity is not only consistent with the presence of this instinct, but, at bottom, requires it. There doubtless can exist creatures of God without such an instinct. But man ceases to be human, unpossessed of such an instinct. Human purity is thus essentially a virtue operating within the body—a fleshly virtue.

Yet Mr. F. R. Tennant's books, so wholesomely suggestive on this point, should suffice to warn us how easily we can be led on to think of the body as ultimately the occasion of *all* our sins, as well as of our virtues; or, at least, to make impurity be, in our minds, *the* sin, the type and measure of all sin. For, with Tennant, *all* sin is but an *atavism*, a lapse back into the animalism from out of which mankind has raised itself. Impurity is a direct atavism—a gross, simple atavism, whilst *pride* is an indirect atavist—a subtilised, compound animalism. But this, I do not doubt, is a strangely inadequate view, both as to the sheer facts and as to the specifically Christian position. For the facts readily show that the occasions, the effects and the reactions of our consciousness with regard to Impurity, are all different from the occasions, the effects and the reactions of Pride. It is very distinctly *not* the animal within us which does lead us to sloth, gluttony and impurity.

And as to the Christian outlook, its genius is sensitively keen and final concerning which is the central, the most heinous sin. *The central sin, for the Christian, is Pride and Self-sufficiency,* distinctly more so than Impurity and Sloth.

I take the occasion, the very possibility of such pride and self-sufficiency, to spring, not from the body at all, but from the delicate poise of our imperfect freedom. We possess a real, but only partial independence; we own a limited power and a limited self-determinative freedom, and even these our fundamental qualities we owe, not to our own making or finding, but we hold them as gifts, as creations of God. The very deep doctrine of the Fall of the Angels grandly illustrates this position. The Angels are without bodies; yet this does not lift them above probation, but merely makes their testing a testing in Humility instead of Purity. And, again, this absence of bodies does not make the alternatives or the Fall of these Angels to be less. On the contrary, it makes them greater.

I can only say that these two convictions, as to the nature of human Purity, and as to the rank of Humility amongst the virtues of all the creatures of God, have greatly helped my Prayer. For the conviction as to Purity has freed me from much previous scruple and depression : and the conviction as to Humility has, I feel, anchored me more deeply and more securely in the Christian Ideal, in the Christian life, and in the rich Christian fact—the life and spirit of Jesus Christ, our Lord.

6

A right attitude towards Temptation and towards Sin. Such an attitude springs from two vivid perceptions : a keen sense of the difference between Perfect Liberty, as we found it to characterise God, and Imperfect Liberty, as it exists in man and, indeed, doubtless in all the higher and highest creatures of God; and an equally keen sense of how all-penetrating and all-characterising is, for man, the effect of this his Imperfect Liberty. The first sense, as to the Imperfection of our Liberty, will save us, as we have seen, from all pride, not only in our perhaps actually being some kind of Byron or Don Juan, but even in our ability thus to fall away from what we should be. And the second sense, as to the special character conferred upon all our moral and spiritual life by this our betwixt and between position of Imperfect Freedom, will keep us awake to the fact that, for our special human kind and degree of virtue, Temptation is indeed necessary, in the long run and upon the whole, for the perfecting and testing of our moral and spiritual life. Temptation—Temptation to sin—is necessary; but not the Commission of sin, not sin itself.

Both these facts find their supreme illustration in the earthly life of Jesus. His Sinlessness—the unquestioning conviction of His sinlessness—appears in the oldest documents, but also His Temptedness. This temptedness disappears already in the Fourth Gospel. Yet the Synoptic Gospels (especially St. Luke), and the Epistle to the Hebrews, give varied and quite unforced expression to the reality of these temptations and to the primitiveness of the belief in their reality. We thus secure the text: 'He was tempted like unto ourselves in all points, yet without sin.' This, for the Humanity even of Jesus Christ. And we affirm the doctrine 'without Sin, without Temptation, without Suffering'—this, for God—indeed even for the Divinity of Jesus Christ. 'Credo in Deum Impassibilem', declared the Council of Aquileia.

I wish we could all vividly realize how all grave sin, actually committed by us, leaves—at least for and during this our earthly life—scars and limitations upon our souls, even after our most generous penitence. Thus St. Augustine did not simply profit by his sins. They became, indeed, the occasions for a grand humility and for the keenest sense of the mercy of God. He became, in spite of his past sins, a greater Saint than is many another saint whose sins were far fewer or far smaller. But Augustine the Sinner, even when he had become Augustine the Penitent, did not surpass, not even equal what—everything else being equal— would have been Augustine the Innocent. He would then, for instance, not have so closely grazed Gnosticism in his treatment of marriage. So, too, the noble founder of La Trappe, the vehement de Rancé, did not simply profit all round by his former sins, heroically repented of though they were. His aversion to all critical historical work, as part of the lives of monks, is doubtless an excess, and an excess which forms part of the reaction from his former worldly life. Here, too, the model of all models is Jesus Christ Our Lord—Jesus, and not even St. Paul. Our Lord's Humanity really grows and grows 'in favour with God and man' amidst real temptation. But Jesus commits no sin; nor is there any trace of a reaction, still less of any excessive reaction, from a sinful life, or, indeed, from any single sin. And this Sinlessness does not spell weakness, but the fullest power.

Let us penetrate our prayer with these discriminations, and let us beware of loose thinking about the profitableness of sin, which, alas, even great poets such as Robert Browning have, at times, encouraged. I am very sure that, if we keep persistently awake to the contrast between ourselves, the tempted and sinning, and Jesus, the sinless but tempted, and again God, the living Reality beyond all sin and temptation, we shall greatly strengthen and fruitfully articulate our prayer.

7

The Divinely intended End of our Life is Joy overflowing and infinite, a Joy closely connected with a noble asceticism.

There is a wholesome, a strengthening *zest* attached to all action which is right and appropriate for the agent; and there is unhealthily weakening *excitement*, which accompanies or follows all activity that is wrong or inappropriate. Hence one great end, and one sure test of right living and right disposition, is the degree to which such living and dispositions make zest to prevail in our lives and make excitement to disappear from them. Now there is no zest comparable to the zest, the expansion, the joy brought to the soul by God and the soul's close union with Him. True, here below, we require to the end a filial reverence, fear, restraint; virtues which, in the beyond, will continue deepened, in the life of Adoration. True, again, we must never cease to fight Self, to flee from Self. 'The love of God, even to the contempt of self,' must more and more supplant the 'love of self, even to the contempt of God.' We never may directly seek mere pleasure. Yet it is also true that we possess, deep within us, a spontaneous affinity for God. Nature draws us to God, as the dim, though most real background and groundwork of our existence: and Supernature raises this semi-conscious affinity to an active hunger for direct and clear vision, for a true participation in the Supernatural Life of God. Hence we must, in our practice, beware of deciding, as to what precisely to think, to do, to be, in execution of God's will for us, directly and simply in favour of what we do not like, or what we like least. We ought, instead, quietly to concentrate our thoughts upon God—upon His will and His various calls, and upon discovering which of such forms and degrees of moral and spiritual life most draws the soul in the moments of its greatest clearness and peacefulness, as to what is somehow meant for it. There will be plenty of opportunities for a large and deep asceticism within the life thus chosen, when we come, as assuredly we will, to have patiently to hold out, and laboriously to advance along the road—a road which, nevertheless will be *the* road to Peace and to Power for the chooser.

We will not, of course, rule out, for ourselves or for others, the practice, or at least the spirit, also of bodily austerities. The spirit, and even some mild amount of the actual practice, of such austerities is, indeed, an integral constituent of all virile religion : the man who laughs at the plank bed and the discipline is a shallow fool. Indeed, some souls are, undoubtedly, called to more than the minimum indicated, and only find their full peace and persuasiveness in some such bodily asceticism. Thus there was a Sacred Heart nun, of whom I heard some time ago, who dearly loved, and anxiously watched over one of the pupils of the convent school, a beautiful young woman. This young woman, soon after leaving the school, took to an evil life and became a wealthy man's mistress. The nun knew well how unavailing would be, in this case, any direct appeal to the girl's religion or conscience. So she wrote to the girl that she was sure the girl loved her and wished her to live for many a year. Well, she merely wanted the girl to know that, on every day during which this her immoral life should last, she, the nun, would scourge herself till her feet stood in a pool of her own blood. That she had already carried out this plan daily since she knew of the girl's condition; and that nothing could or would stop her but the girl's own written announcement that she had left the man. The days went by. At last the girl wrote. The nun had gained her point. Is not this grand?

Yet it is Love, God, that first should be in our hearts; and if that Love then impels us to such deeds, we will attempt to do them, to feed and to express our Love of that Love, and not otherwise. There is an admirable letter on asceticism generally from Fénelon to Madame de Maintenon. My own daughter, a Carmelite nun, spoke simply the spirit of her great Order, when, some little time ago, she answered an Anglican married lady, who declared herself repelled by all such mortifications—how could they ever form a part of the Christian life? Did not God Himself send us crosses, sufficient for all purposes, through and within our duties? Why arbitrarily add to these? The nun answered that she did not, indeed, find any trace of an *attrait* to such mortifications in her questioner—let her cheerfully leave such things alone and serve God joyfully along her way. That these things are never more than instruments or applications of the one spirit and way of love and of service. But that the lady would be unwise did she go further—if she condemned all such things for everyone. God's calls, within our one great common vocation,

are many and various. Souls exist which are as truly called to such
mortifications, as her soul was *not* called to them. Who are we,
to lay down the law and the limit to God?

In either of these two paths, as Denifle draws out finely in his
great Luther book, the general direction, the End and the Measure are the same—the love of God above all things and the love
of our neighbour as ourselves. And this love of God, where un-
inhibited and full, brings joy—it seeks God, Joy; and it finds Joy,
God. I used to wonder, in my intercourse with John Henry
Newman, how one so good, and who had made so many sacrifices
to God, could be so depressing. And again, twenty years later, I
used to marvel contrariwise, in my intercourse with Abbé
Huvelin, how one more melancholy in natural temperament
than even Newman himself, and one physically ill in ways and
degrees in which Newman never was, could so radiate spiritual
joy and expansion as, in very truth, the Abbé did. I came to feel
that Newman had never succeeded in surmounting his deeply
predestinarian, Puritan, training; whilst Huvelin had nourished
his soul, from boyhood upwards, on the Catholic spirituality as
it flowered in St. Francis. Under the fine rule by which the
Roman Church tribunals require, for Canonization as distinct
from Beatification, that the Servant of God concerned should be
proved to have possessed and to have transmitted a deep spiritual joy, Newman, I felt and feel, could indeed be beatified, but
only Huvelin could be canonized.

Our prayer will greatly benefit by the great facts and discriminations we have been considering. Without in any way
forcing, or escaping from, our real *attrait*, our prayer will thus
possess a double virile asceticism. We shall feel ourselves, even
if personally not called to very definite or to large bodily mortifications, in spiritual touch with, and supplemented by, those
who are; and, again, we will deliberately hold ourselves as
pledged to much renunciation of facile pleasures, as the condition
and cost of our own abiding joy.

EA2, pp. 217–242

Chapter V

A MIXED PASTURE ON PRAYER

I N the following extracts on prayer and the life of sanctity, von Hügel's grasp of the central and deepest of all forms of prayer that is to be found in the mystical experience is never concealed, and it was this which drew him to Catherine of Genoa. But when this has been said, it is always the flowing out of this prayer into the full life in this world and the use of the frictional material which comes from this world to drive us even more deeply into the life of prayer, which is von Hügel's distinctive contribution. The autobiographical account of how he came to write on Catherine of Genoa, the saint who spent twenty-five years of her life after her deepest experiences, administering in a hospital and meeting the crises of plagues, brings out with clarity the sources of von Hügel's attraction to her.

Religion, at least among the mystics (and I believe that, on this point at least, the mystics merely dive deeper into and bring out more explicitly the sap or the central core of the religious passion), consists centrally in the sense of Presence—the sense of an overflowing Existence distinct from our own and in the Adoration of the same. True, this Presence, this Existence, is apprehend as All-Good, as Beatific because All-Good.

RG, p. 71

The mystical *élan* ... is essentially a plunge right away from all the other and lesser experience—an act of abandonment into the *drawing*, the attraction of God, and God, reached thus by this severance and by this plunge, then gives the soul a starting-point for such loves of earthly things and persons as may be there to love. The historical-institutional instinct and conception moves from man to God, the mystical attitude moves from God to man.

RG, p. 92

And, at the moment she (Catherine of Genoa) was on her
knees before Him, her heart was pierced by so sudden and so
immense a love of God, accompanied by so penetrating a sight
of her miseries and sins and of His goodness, that she was
near falling to the ground. . . . She saw the offended One to be
supremely good, and the offender quite the opposite. And hence
she could not bear to see any part of herself which was not sub-
jected to the divine justice, with a view of its being thoroughly
chastised.

ME 1, pp. 105, 124

Born as I was in Italy, certain early impressions have never
left me; a vivid consciousness has been with me, almost from
the first, of the massively virile personalities, the spacious, trust-
ful times of the early, as yet truly Christian, Renaissance there,
from Dante on to the Florentine Platonists. And when, on growing up, I acquired strong and definite religious convictions it was
that ampler pre-Protestant, as yet neither Protestant nor anti-
Protestant, but deeply positive and Catholic, world, with its
already characteristically modern outlook and its hopeful and
spontaneous application of religion to the pressing problems of
life and thought, which helped to strengthen and sustain me,
when depressed and hemmed in by the types of devotion prevalent since then in Western Christendom. For those early
modern times presented me with men of the same general
instinct and outlook as my own, but environed by the priceless
boon and starting-point of a still undivided Western Christendom;
Protestantism, as such, continued to be felt as ever more or
less unjust and sectarian; and the specifically post-Tridentine
type of Catholicism, with its regimental Seminarism, its predominantly controversial spirit, its suspiciousness and timidity,
persisted, however inevitable some of it may be, in its failure to
win my love. Hence I had to continue the seeking and the finding
elsewhere, yet ever well within the great Roman Church, things
more intrinsically lovable. The wish some day to portray one
of those large-souled pre-Protestant, post-Mediaeval Catholics,
was thus early and has been long at work within me.

And then came John Henry Newman's influence with his
Dream of Gerontius, and a deep attraction to St. Catherine of
Genoa's doctrine of the soul's self-chosen, intrinsic purification;
and much lingering about the scenes of Caterinetta's life and
labours, during more than twenty stays in her terraced city that

looks away so proudly to the sea. Such a delicately psychological, soaring, yet sober-minded Eschatology, with its striking penetration and unfolding of the soul's central life and alternatives as they are already here and now, seemed to demand an ampler study than it had yet received, and to require a vivid presentation of the noble, strikingly original personality from whom it sprang. . . .

The wish arose to utilize, as fully as possible, this long, close contact with a soul of most rare spiritual depth—a soul that presents, with an extraordinary, provocative vividness, the greatness, helps, problems and dangers of the mystical spirit. I now wanted to try and get down to the driving forces of this kind of religion, and to discover in what way such a keen sense of, and absorption in, the Infinite can still find room for the Historical and Institutional elements of Religion, and, at the same time, for that noble concentration upon not directly religious contingent facts and happenings, and upon laws of causation or of growth, which constitutes the scientific temper of mind and its specific, irreplaceable duties and virtues. Thus, having begun to write a biography of St. Catherine, with some philosophical elucidations, I have finished by writing an essay on the philosophy of Mysticism, illustrated by the life of Caterinetta Fiesca Adorna and her friends.

ME 1, pp. xxi–xxiii

It has been well said that there are three stages of the spiritual life, and three corresponding classes of souls. There are the souls that are characterized, even to the end of their earthly lives, by that, more or less complete, naturalistic Individualism, with which we all in various degrees begin. Catherine's own time and country were full of such thoroughly Individualistic, unmoral or even anti-moral men, who, however gifted and cultivated as artists, scholars, philosophers, and statesmen, must yet be counted as essentially childish and as clever animals rather than as spiritual men. And she herself had, during the five years which had preceded her conversion, tended, on the surface of her being, towards something of this kind.

Next come the souls that have recognised and have accepted Duty and Obligation, that are now striving to serve God as God, and that are attempting, with a preponderant sincerity, to live the common and universal life of the Spirit. These of necessity tend to suspect, or even to suppress and sacrifice, whatever appears to be peculiar to themselves, as so much individualistic subjectivity and insidious high treason to the objective law of Him who made their souls, and who now bids them save those souls at any cost. The large majority of the souls that were striving to serve God in Catherine's times belonged, as souls belong in these our days, and will necessarily and rightly belong up to the end, to this second, universalistic, uniformative type and class. And Catherine herself evidently belonged prominently to this type and class, during her first four convert years.

And there are, finally, an ever relatively small number of souls that are called, and a still smaller number that attain, to a state in which the University, Obligation, Uniformity and Objectivity, of the second stage and class, take the form of a Spiritual Individuality, Liberty, Variety and Subjectivity : Personality in the fullest sense of the term has now appeared. And this fullest Spiritual Personality is the profoundest opposite and foe of its naturalistic counterfeit, of those spontaneous animal liberalisms which reigned, all but unrecognised as such because all but uncontrasted by the true ideal and test of life, prior to that prostration before absolute obligation, that poignant sense of weakness and impurity, and that gain of strength and purity from beyond its furthest reaches, experienced by the soul at its conversion. . . .

Catherine attained unmistakably, after her four years of special penitence, to this rare third stage. For not only is she essentially as individual and unique as if she were not universal and uniform; and essentially as universal and uniform as if she were not individual : but she is indefinitely more truly original and subjective, because of her voluntary boundness and objectivity. Indeed she is solidly and really free and personal, because the continuous renunciation and expulsion of all naturalistic individuality remains, to the very end, one of the essential functions of her soul.

ME 1, pp. 241–243

The deeply dramatic character of the spiritual life consists largely in the way in which even the most spiritual consolations flee from the soul which seeks them directly as such, and the manner in which the deepest consolations will, on the contrary, come to the soul that seeks directly only God and His will, whether sweet or bitter, or even God and only suffering for His sake.

Only the pure of heart shall see God; only the contrite and broken heart will not be despised by God. Yet it remains true that, although we must not directly seek joy out of relation to God, yet joy follows upon our thus seeking God first and our seeking all in Him; joy and God at bottom are essentially interconnected, indeed the ultimate, alone sufficing joy is God Himself and the touch of His closer union with our souls; and it is only because of our weakness and cowardice, which so readily shrinks from the times when we have to pay for such joy and sinks to pleasures in themselves, that persistent precaution is necessary for the soul against inverting, in its practice, the objective order and proportion as we find them in the lives of the Saints.

RG, p. 104

Thus I came to see with my own children that, as they all grew up, they understood what I meant by a certain pang being necessary for the soul which would really grow—a pang, or a very real jealousy, when it has for the first time clearly to recognize not simply its inferiority to this or that soul here and now, with the possibility of after all catching up that soul or even doing better than that soul, but to recognize, and that with joy and gratitude to God, that it never will, that it never can be the equal, still less the superior of that soul in God's heaven, the home of many mansions. And I came to see how for oneself this pang would come again and again, and yet how good it was for one to be made thus to see one's meanness, how good to be made to feel that there was something within one like even to God and especially to His goodness, His kind of goodness, a goodness which could not be other than it is, a goodness which is essentially Joy and Beatitude throughout.

RG, pp. 123–124

God is a Reality immeasurably more important than are we ourselves; He is the only genuinely central reality extant, so that we have always to end by seeing ourselves as His effects or His permissions or as so many freedoms of a limited kind usable by us, through His mysterious allowance, even to a certain extent against Himself. The centre of the picture has thus to be God and not ourselves, although only where we make ourselves the centre of the picture is the picture then and there clear. But then it would be our own fault, our own poverty of experience or imagination or of power to state the facts as known by us, if that egocentric position were not promptly seen to be the most intolerable of self-imprisonments.

RG, pp. 135–136

Religion, indeed, has ever been, at its fullest and deepest, *Adoration,* hence apprehension and affirmation of, and joy in, what already *is*; and the Prevenience of God, His part in the religious act, has consequently, by the Prophets and Psalmists, by Jesus and St. Paul, by St. Augustine and Pascal, been dwelt upon almost to the exclusion of our own part. Kant, as usual, seizes the central difficulty here, and rightly rejects exclusively divine acts within our souls; doubtless the Divine Action must be conceived as ever inviting our own, and as, where an act pleasing to God is the result, ever accompanied by some human, presumably our own, activity. Yet that divine environment and prevenience, the all-in-all of God, Who Himself has deigned to limit Himself in order to leave to us the kind and degree of liberty He has chosen for us; the great fact, not of our own action, but of what renders that action possible, especially in forms and with motives too high and too wide for the world of simple sense or of unaided nature : these are the realities and truths central to the religious consciousness.

EL, pp. 160–161

A Benedictine Bee-keeper, who has loved and watched the ways of bees for now some thirty years, told me in vivid detail how much circumspection precedes the final straight, bee-line flight to their far-away collecting ground. He has stood, how often! to watch especially the young start their day's work at sunrise. The bee would rise straight up into the air for some fifty feet or so; it there would remain on poise for quite an appreciable time prospecting, circumspecting, taking mysterious bearings all around; and only when it had quite finished this, its leisurely mustering of the situation, would it fly off, but now without the slightest hesitation, intermittence or deflection, to the clover field or heather common or clematis hedgerow some two miles away. Let this little fact and story be to us all a symbol and reminder of the temper and the procedure which, I am very sure, are alone right and promising in the difficult, delicate task before us. Perhaps we may be able to fly straight, to alight plumb upon the solution, the rich system of facts and of reality we are seeking; but, assuredly, we can finish thus only if we begin differently—only if we start, and indeed continue long, in care, poise, and cautious circumspection.

EA 2, p. 167

Though the soul cannot abidingly abstract itself from its fellows, it can and ought frequently to recollect itself in a simple sense of God's presence. Such moments of direct preoccupation with God alone bring a deep refreshment and simplification to the soul.

EL, p. 396

In Mainz Cathedral, presumably on his way to Vienna, an incident occurred which had a profound effect on him. Standing in the dark recesses of the building, he (von Hügel) saw a young woman rush in. From the disorder of her dress he gathered that she was a mother who had been nursing her baby and from the agony of her expression and the violence of her sobs, he realized that the baby had just died. He shrank behind a pillar. She ran up the church and threw herself before the High Altar. Her sobs gradually quietened and silence followed. As she came back down the church, he saw her face, and it was radiant. From that moment all his doubts about the efficacy of prayer were ended.

B, p. 18

Drop brain, open wide the soul, nourish the heart, purify, strengthen the will: with this, you are sure to grow; without this, you are certain to shrink.

How much you can learn, as I myself have learnt, from watching cattle dreamily grazing and ruminating in their pastures! See how the sagacious creatures, without any theory or inflation of mind, instinctively select the herbs and grasses that suit and sustain them; and how they peacefully pass by what does not thus help them! They do not waste their time and energy in tossing away, or in trampling upon, or even simply in sniffing at, what is anti-pathetic to them. Why should they? Thistles may not suit *them*; well there are other creatures in the world whom thistles *do* suit. And, in any case, are they the police of this rich and varied universe?

EA, p. 99

Chapter VI

ALL HIGH RELIGION HAS THREE DIMENSIONS

THIS next set of spiritual counsels repeats and reaffirms what was noted in connection with his advices on the life of prayer. He seems to find his task that of creating a climate which is congenial to the practice of a rich religious life in our time. In the first place this means an acknowledgment that the individual soul needs a religious community: a church, and that no ultramodern situation can ever render this element of religion obsolete. But to live in our world means that the religious man must come to terms with the scientific world and with the intellectual element of religion itself. Von Hügel's notion of the role of science to the religious man as an ascetic element—a contemporary form of asceticism—is an original and fascinating suggestion which was buttressed by his own practice not alone of the handicraft of bookbinding, but also of geology and of textual criticism and by their effects on his own religious life.

Throughout these counsels he seeks to expand and deepen personal religious experience, not by replacing it, for he knows it to be the core of religion, but by making it aware of its immeasurable need for and debt to both the scientific-intellectual and the institutional-historical factors. Always the enemy lurking inside religion, according to von Hügel, is an absolutizing tendency marked by oversimplification and leading to a narrow impoverishment and to a flight into watertight compartments within the mind. The invitation which he offers is to precisely the opposite. It is to a religion that is inwardly secure in the richness of its inward experience at the center and therefore very free at the periphery.

I should like to show the complexity special to the deepest kind of life, to Religion; and to attempt some description of the working harmonization of this complexity. If Religion turned out to be simple, in the sense of being a monotone, a mere oneness, a whole without parts, it could not be true; and yet if Religion be left too much a mere multiplicity, a mere congeries of parts without a whole, it cannot be persuasive and fully operative. And the several constituents are there, whether we harbour, recognize, and discipline them or not; but these constituents will but hinder or supplant each other, in proportion as they are not somehow each recognized in their proper place and rank, and are not each allowed and required to supplement and to stimulate the other.

ME 1, p. 50

Religion is at all times more or less both traditional and individual; both external and internal; both institutional, rational, and volitional. It always answers more or less to the needs of authority and society; of reason and proof; of interior sustenance and purification. I believe because I am told, because it is true, because it answers to my deepest interior experiences and needs. And, everything else being equal, my faith will be at its richest and deepest and strongest, in so far as all these motives are most fully and characteristically operative within me, at one and the same time, and towards one and the same ultimate result and end.

Now all this is no fancy scheme, no petty or pretty artificial arrangement: the danger and yet necessity of the presence of these three forces, the conflicts and crises within and between them all, in each human soul, and between various men and races that typify or espouse one or the other force to the more or less complete exclusion of the other, help to form the deepest history, the truest tragedy or triumph of the secret life of every one of us.

The crisis is perilous. For he (the religious man) will be greatly tempted either to cling exclusively to his existing, all but simply institutional, external position, and to fight or elude all approaches to its reasoned, intellectual apprehension and systematization; and in this case his religion will tend to contract and shrivel up, and to become a something simply alongside of other things in his life. Or he will feel strongly pressed to let the individually intellectual simply supplant the institutional, in which case his religion will grow hard and shallow, and will tend to disappear altogether. In the former case he will, at best, assimilate his religion to external law and order, to Economics and Politics; in the latter case he will, at best, assimilate it to Science and Philosophy. In the first case, he will tend to superstition; in the second, to rationalism and indifference.

But even if he passes well through this first crisis, and has thus achieved the collaboration of these two religious forces, the external and the intellectual, his religion will still be incomplete and semi-operative, because still not reaching to what is deepest and nearest to his will. A final transition, the addition of the third force, that of the emotional-experimental life, must yet be safely achieved. And this again is perilous: for the two other forces will, even if single, still more if combined, tend to appear as akin to revolution; to the intellectual side it will readily seem mere subjectivity and sentimentality ever verging on delusion. And the emotional-experimental force will, in its turn, be tempted to sweep aside both the external, as so much oppressive ballast; and the intellectual, as so much hair-splitting or rationalism. And if it succeeds, a shifting subjectivity, and all but incurable tyranny of mood and fancy, will result,—fanaticism is in full sight.

ME 1, pp. 51–55

Now the tendency of a soul, when once awake to this necessary freshness and interiority of feeling with regard to God's and her own action, will again be towards an impoverishing oneness. It will now tend to shrink away from the External, Institutional altogether. For though it cannot but have experienced the fact that it was by contact with this External that, like unto Antaeus at his contact with Mother Earth, it gained its experience of the Internal, yet each such experience tends to obliterate the traces of its own occasion. Indeed the interior feeling thus achieved tends, in the long run, to make the return to the contact with the fact that occasioned, and to the act that produced it, a matter of effort and repugnance. It seems a case of 'a man's returning to his mother's womb'; and is indeed a new birth to a fuller life, and hence humiliating, obscure, concentrated, effortful, a matter of trust and labour and pain and faith and love,—a true death of, and adieu to the self of this moment, however advanced this self may seem,—a fully willed purifying pang. Only through such dark and narrow Thermopylae passes can we issue on to the wide, sunlit plains. And both plain and sunshine can never last long at a time: and they will cease altogether, if they are not interrupted by this apparent shadow of the valley of death, this concrete action, which invariably modifies not only the soul's environment, but above all the soul itself.

Thus, in all these cases, this feeling will rapidly lead the soul on to become unconsciously weak or feverish, unless the soul manfully escapes from this feeling's tyranny, and nobly bends under the yoke and cramps itself within the narrow limits of the life-giving concrete act. The Church's insistence upon *some* vocal prayer, upon *some* definite, differentiated, specific acts of the various moral and theological virtues, upon Sacramental practice throughout all the states and stages of the Christian life, is but a living commentary upon the difficulty and importance of the point under discussion. And History, as we have seen, confirms all this.

ME 1, pp. 73–74

Never has religion been purely and entirely individual; always has it been, as truly and necessarily, social and institutional, traditional and historical. And this traditional element, not all the religious genius in the world can ever escape or replace: it was there, surrounding and moulding the very pre-natal existence of each one of us; it will be there, long after we have left the scene. We live and die its wise servants and stewards, or its blind slaves, or in futile, impoverishing revolt against it: we never, for good or for evil, really get beyond its reach.

ME 1, pp. 59–60

... All sane and full Epistemology, and all the more complete, characteristic and fruitful religious experiences and personalities imperatively demand, in the writer's judgement, some genuine Institutionalism. ... If man's spirit is awakened by contact with the things of sense, and if his consciousness of the Eternal and the Omnipresent is aroused and (in the long run) sustained only by the aid of Happenings in Time and in Space, then the Historical, Institutional, Sacramental must be allowed a necessary position and function in the full religious life. No cutting of knots however difficult, no revolt against, no evasion of abuses however irritating or benumbing, are adequate solutions. Only the proper location, the heroic use, the wise integration of the Institutional within the full spiritual life are really sufficient.

EL, pp. xiv–xv

The late Dr. James Martineau, the well-known Unitarian preacher and philosopher, had allowed me to come and see him, for the first time and the last, in his rarely tidy study in his house in Gordon Square. He was then over ninety years of age; yet bolt upright he sat, slim of figure, faultlessly neat, clean-shaven, clear-eyed, keen of speech, vivid in mind, utterly youthful and ardent of soul, there—the fine, aspiring man—before me. And, as the finish of our long talk, he told me the following experience of his:

In that chair in which you sit, there sat, not many weeks ago, a man whose case will, surely, interest you as much as it has interested myself. Not much over a year ago I was first visited by this man, then quite unknown to me, even by name, and who came, without presentation of any kind, and simply asked to be allowed to see me. The man was an American, in his middle thirties, of vigorous health, spirits and will, of university training and considerable culture—a man of wealth and leisure. He sat in your chair there, and, that first time, said he had long known me in America by repute and from my writings as an honest man—as a believer, it is true, but as a believer in not over-much. And since he was now perplexed and in want of sound advice, he had just come straight from America to Europe and this room in order to consult me, and, if possible, to act on my suggestions. That, after taking his degree, he had found himself free to do with his life whatsoever he might think most useful and pressing for himself and others. That he was at that time, not only without any religious belief, but full of the most complete, contemptuous conviction that religion is utterly illusionist and thoroughly mischievous. Hence he decided to devote all his time and strength to the systematic eradication of religion. He had now a record of ten years behind him, during which the weekdays had been spent in preparing the unhesitating assaults of his Sunday lay-sermons. That he had, from first to last, very great success—at least of the more tangible kinds: wherever he went there were crowded meetings, cordial receptions, apparently unhesitating acceptance. And nothing that he could trace or name had happened within his own personal life to make himself hesitate at all. And yet, he knew not how or why, he had now for some months become pursued by the suggestions, as of so many whispers: 'Is it not possible that, after all, you are mistaken? How can you be so utterly sure that all the various religions, also in what they all affirm, are purely, foolishly, demonstrably deluded? Why not suspend your propaganda for a little? Why not re-study the whole question in a more leisurely, a wider, a new frame of mind? Why not at least get away to Europe—procure an opinion as to what to do and how to act?' And so there he now had come to me, and he would ask me: 'What would you, Dr. Martineau, yourself do in such a case as mine?'

And Dr. Martineau then proceeded: 'I told him, after careful reflection' (I suppose Dr. Martineau asked the American to return after some days), 'that the following is what I myself would do. Let him give twice six months to the following double experiment and analysis. Let both half-years be spent by himself each time exclusively amongst members of one and the same race: the first six months amongst the most traditionally and still unbrokenly believing and practising persons of this race, bereft of all the charm of intellectual culture, quick-wittedness, breadth of sympathy, modern elasticity; the second six months amongst the persons most emancipated from all such religious traditions and convictions, but full of all the charm of intellectual culture, quick-wittedness, breadth of outlook, ceaseless mobility and elasticity of mind. The first six months will best be spent in a Westphalian peasant family—Roman Catholic unbrokenly for well a thousand years; and the second six months shall be spent, equally exclusively amidst the medical students of Berlin, full of the flux of our day. Thus the difference of race will be eliminated, and also the possibility of, on either side, being bribed against his better judgment. And, when he had quite finished his twice six months' immersions, let him ask himself sincerely, whether either group, and if one of them, then which, possessed that deep mysterious thing, the secret, the wisdom of life—which group knew, operatively, the meaning of birth, of suffering, of passion, of sin, of joy, of death. And let him come and report the upshot to him, Dr. Martineau, in this same room.'

'Well, the American carried out this entire programme, and there, in your chair, he sat again quite recently, and reported his conclusions to me. He had lived long enough immersed in the atmosphere and experiences of each group, to have lived with each through a birth, a death, a grave moral lapse— troubles, sufferings, successes of various sudden or sullen kinds. The Catholic peasant group had been rough and clumsy, narrow in its sympathies, full of prejudice even against orthodox Protestants, and quite incapable of conceiving a modern

doubt or difficulty as anything but so much pride or impurity.
They were always treading on his corns, and were full of little
practices, superstition, magic. The sceptical medical group
had been polished and supple, open to anything provided it
were but new or spelt revolt, full of encouragement to every
scepticism, sure everywhere that it was manly and true. These
men were always soothing and anticipating all his tastes and
fancies; and as to religious practices or scruples, they had, of
course, simply none. And yet, and yet! When face to face
with those grim realities of life, those clumsy, "superstitious,"
narrow Popish peasants possessed a depth of insight, an assurance of action, an at-homeness of conviction, of a magnificent
swiftness, purity and massiveness. And, when face to face
with these same realities, the nimble "enlightened" materialist
students were utterly helpless, without insight, action, conviction of any kind. The contrast and difference was clear,
decisive. Should he ever again lose this sense of the unspeak-
able superiority possessed, in what supremely matters, by those
traditional believing Westphalians over these individualist
sceptical Berliners?'

And Dr. Martineau finished by telling me how he said to this
young man:

'Now, look you—you have received a great grace from God,
a light which you must carefully guard and conscientiously
follow, or it will dwindle and go out. Return to America now,
but courageously re-start, reform your life to the degree and
the kind which your experiences may now tell your conscience clearly that you ought thus to change. You know well
that I am no Roman Catholic. I shall be glad if you shall find
yourself not obliged, in conscience to identify, for your own
self, a deep faith in God and a devoted life in Him and for
Him with Roman Catholicism. But pray understand me well:
did I find myself in my conscience forced to choose between God
and the Pope, and no Pope, indeed, but also no God—no fervent,
devoted service of God, of Christ, of souls—then, without a
moment's hesitation, I would choose, as I would in such a case
wish yourself to choose, not no God no Pope—even Pope—
and God.'

EA 2, pp. 126–129

There is, again, no such thing for man as a complete escape from history and institutions. Thus the Quakers, very wisely, possess the institution of the Meetings of the First Day and of their strict obligation. Indeed the minor religious bodies are generally characterised by the specially emphatic stress laid by them upon some, or all, of the few institutions retained by them. We can thus maintain without undue paradox, that, by appurtenance to a particular religious body, we really keep in touch with the great tradition of mankind at large, and with God's general action in individual souls. And there is, finally, no such thing as appurtenance to a particular religious body without cost—cost to the poorer side of human nature and cost even, in some degree and way, to the better side of that same nature. Hence the need of an increasingly wise discrimination—of a generous payment of the cost where it affects the poorer side, and of a careful limitation of the cost, and a resourceful discovery of compensation elsewhere, where the cost affects the better side of our nature.

EA, p. 15

And, in Religion in particular, it is useless to argue that, God being everywhere, what need have we of special places for His worship? It is man who worships, not God; but man, here below at least, experiences in space as he does in time; one place is not the same to him as another place, any more than one time is the same to him as another time. Cease to worship God in particular places, and your worship will become less vivid, less concentrated.

EA 2, p. 67

Where we cannot trace the Institutional Element in a soul's life, we always find either that this soul's religion has constantly been weak; or that the soul is suffering under a reaction from some religious excess, and is losing its religion; or that it is in the process of gaining some institutionalism; or finally, that its religion, though non-institutional is indeed delicate and deep, but that this religion was first awakened in this soul by some fervent Institutional religionist. We certainly find the Institutional at work ... in the great Israelitish and Jewish prophets; in our Lord and the Apostles, especially St. Paul; in Origen, Augustine and Aquinas; but also in Luther and Calvin; especially again in St. Theresa, in Pascal, Bossuet, Fénelon; and in Laud

Lancelot Andrewes, and William Law. And again in such modern
Philosophers as Nicholas of Cusa, Leibnitz and Berkeley....
The same element of Institutionalism is of course observable in
post-Christian Judaism, in Mohammedanism, in Brahminism, in
Buddhism.

EL, pp. 325–326

... It is in the contact, as close and penetrating as possible
with the concrete, with history, with institutions, with social
groups, that men are most fully awakened to and steadied in
the sense of the Unconditioned, the Abiding, the Prevenient, the
Beginning and the End and Crown of light and life and love. If
this is so, historical and institutional forms of religion, or rather
the historical and institutional element which always appears
promptly in religion, must be a most important constituent of
the whole....

RG, p. 18

What happens in the normal, that is in the historical and
institutional religious life, is that, during the periods of obscurity,
the soul lives in a very true sense in the faith of its fellows until
fresh light makes it in its turn support the others. No man is
sufficient to himself, not in shoemaking, not in printing, not in
advertising: it is only in the deepest of all things, in religion,
that we hear men talk and write, more often than is pleasant, as
though it were sufficient for them to cut themselves off from
all others to think and to write good sense.

RG, p. 144

... I can remember quite plainly that already then, at five
and six years of age, I possessed a sense, not only of God in the
eternal, especially the organic, world, but of a mysterious divine
Presence in the churches of Florence. Thus historical religion
was with me, together with metaphysical (and natural) religion,
from the first.

RG, p. 80

Man's capacity of attention and of persistent operative interest is essentially limited; and only great, unbroken traditions of
spiritual experience and of mental training are, in ordinary circumstances, able somewhat to extend these limits. But those

great traditions are, for the most part, practically unknown in the world we are now considering.

EL, p. 307

First, then, official organisation and authority are part, a normally necessary part, of the fuller and more fruitful religious life; but they are ever only a part, and a part in what is a dynamic whole—one movement and moment in what is a life, in the deepest sense of the word. The lonely, new and daring (if but faithful, reverent and loving) outgoing of the discoverer and investigator are as truly acts of, are as necessary parts of, the Church and her life as his coming back to the Christian hive and community, which latter will then gradually test his contribution by tentative applications to its own life, and will in part assimilate, in part simply tolerate, in part finally reject it. And such a lonely, venturesome outgoing appears, in all kinds of degree and form, in every sort of life. The inventive, often most daring, ever at first opposed, philanthropy of the Saints belongs entirely to this exploratory, pioneer class of action in the rhythmic 'inspiration-expiration' life, in the breathing of the living Church. The Church is thus, ever and everywhere, both progressive and conservative; both reverently free-lance and official; both as it were male and female, creative and reproductive; both daring to the verge of presumption, and prudent to the verge of despair.

EA 2, pp. 16–17

Yet, upon close examination, we always discover that, be the abuses or errors on Tradition's side ever so heavy, *some* Tradition not only remains necessary, but is operating most powerfully, as a positive ingredient and shaping power, within even the most independent-seeming, the most anti-traditional utterances of any Prophet that ever lived.

EA 2, p. 67

And lastly, Eternal Life will not be simply a Moralism, with just the addition of a theoretical or practical reference to God, as the sanction and source of morality. Such a Religion has, fortunately, never existed except in the heads of some Philosophers. In its central consciousness and action, this Life will be indeed religious, hence Adoration, a Cultus—a deep, rich, spiritual Cultus, but a Cultus still. This for the ingoing, recollective

movement. And the outgoing movement will not only discover God as hidden in the deepest ideals, necessities, and im-
pulsions of Ethics, but also in the fullest strivings of Art in the
widest and most delicate attempts of the speculative and
analytical reason. God is no less truly the ultimate Source, Sus-
tainer, and End of perfect Beauty and of utter Truth than of
complete Goodness and of the purest Self-Donation.

EL, p. 392

For if by Mysticism we mean a doctrine or method which
bids us fly, as constantly and as much as possible, from contact
and conflict with the contingent and the relative, from the local
and temporal concrete, from the historical, visible, and institutional, and carefully to seek and to keep Truth and Life in the
abstract and but-thinkable; then no position could well be less
mystical than the one here advanced. For here the vivid sense of
the Absolute and the Abiding are considered to appear within
our lives always in contrast with, and as a spontaneous and
necessary concomitant and condition of, our apprehension of
the Contingent and the Finite. And since our minds would be as
unable to acquire or to long retain any vivid sense of the Absolute and of God, separately and alone, as to do without that
sense: this position would insist upon the most regular, patient,
precise and loyally docile contact, conflict and labour with and
at the Contingent. Only in the shock between finite mind and
finite fact, like cold steel striking against cold flint, does the
latent fire of all true life spring forth for a moment; only in the
patient pressure applied by the mind to these dusty-looking facts,
like dry hands pressing a seemingly, empty sponge, are the
hidden waters of life wrung from the arid givenness of the Contingent. It is as though we became aware of a broad-stretching,
mist-covered lake, only on occasion of the leaping of some fish
upon its surface, and of the momentary glimpse of the shin-
ing silver. . . .

For in addition to this close contact with the Contingent, in
research and action and suffering, of any and every humble-
noble kind, the soul would have to faithfully cultivate the getting
away again from this outward action, back to interior recollection, silence, aspiration, increased subconsciousness and prayer.
And, indeed, only by such a rhythmic movement would the soul
itself be able to utilise and see the indications and experiences
of the Absolute, which its work called forth: things which

would otherwise, in so far as still leaving any traces in this soul's observable work, be noted and used by other souls more recollected than itself.

'Experience and Transcendence', pp. 27–29.
This essay in English was issued in a mimeographed edition 'For Private Circulation Only' and was never reprinted in any of his volumes.

Such Institutions, then most rightly maintain the Superhuman Claim as essential to religion; they emphasise Religion as essentially Revelation, as man's deepest experience of the ultimate Reality through the action of that Reality Itself,—a Reality which both underlies and crowns all our other, lesser strivings and *givennesses*. And such Institutions, again, most rightly emphasise the great difference in amount, purity, and worth of the spiritual truth and life to be found even within the sincerest and most entirely positive convictions and practices of the several religions of mankind. Here we have two immense services rendered by the higher Religious Institutions to the abiding truths, to the ultimate basis of man's worth; services absolutely without serious parallel, as to their depth and range, in any other quarter.

Yet that superhuman, revelational Religion has, in the rough and tumble of life, and by and for the average institutionalist, been too often conceived as though arising *in vacuo*, and hence as though able, even in the long run, to dispense with, or to starve, the other activities and necessities of man; or, again, as though not only Religion but Theology were a divine communication—as though God Himself communicated intrinsically adequate, mathematically precise formulations of Religion. And thus we get a starving of all that is not directly religious in man or an arrest of theological improvement. We get an insistence upon a direct and decisive jurisdiction, by a deductive theology and institutional administration, over the results of (indeed over the very methods and necessities specific to) man's other activities and apprehensions, in Science and Aesthetics, in Historical Research, Politics and Ethics, and in Philosophy. And in proportion as this is actually effected, Religion becomes bereft of the material, the friction, the witnesses so essential to the health and fruitfulness of man in general and of Religion in particular. The material is lost; for man's full other experiences, which, pressed, yield so firm a foundation for specific Religion, are here prevented from being thus full and from being thus pressed. The friction between Religion and Ethics, and between Theology and Science and Philosophy, so necessary to bring out the fullest powers of each and the deep underlying mutual need which, in the living man, each has of all the others, is eliminated; since all these several activities, except that of the official Theology, have, previous to all possibility of wholesale clashing, been carefully deprived of all their specific weapons of attack and of defence. And the witnesses for religion disappear; for what is a witness who has, by forcible suppressions or modifications of his testimony, been rendered 'safe' beforehand?

EA, pp. 60–61

We religious men will have to develop, *as part of our religion*, the ceaseless sense of its requiring the *nidus*, materials, stimulant, discipline, of the other God-given, non-religious activities, duties, ideals of man, from his physical and psychical necessities up to his aesthetic, political and philosophical aspirations. The autonomy, competition, and criticism of the other centres of life will have thus to become welcome to religion for the sake of religion itself. We religious men again will have to develop, *as part of our religion*, a sense, not simply of the error and evil, but also of the truth and good, in any and every man's religion. We will have to realise, with Cardinal John de Lugo, S.J. (who died in 1660), that the members of the various Christian sects, of the Jewish and Mohammedan communions, and of the non-Christian philosophies, who achieved and achieve their salvation, did and do so in general simply by God's grace aiding their good faith instinctively to concentrate itself upon, and to practise, those elements in the cultus and teaching of their respective sect, communion or philosophy, which are true and good and originally revealed by God.

EA, pp. 62–63

Man will (if he belongs to our time and to our Western races, and is determined fully to utilize our special circumstances, lights and trials, as so many means towards his own spiritualization) have carefully to keep in living touch with that secondary and preliminary reality, the Thing-world, the Impersonal Element, Physical Science and Determinist Law. He will have to pass and repass beneath these Caudine forks; to plunge and to replunge into and through this fiery torrent; and, almost a merely animal individual at the beginning and on this side of such docile bendings and such courageous plungings, he will (if he combines them with, and effects them through, those two other, abiding and ultimate, directly religious convictions) straighten himself up again to greater heights, and will come forth from the torrent each time a somewhat purer and more developed spiritual person than he was before such contraction and purgation.

ME 2, pp. 378–379

For Religion, in its deepest orientation and need, requires Asceticism, in some form or other; it requires touch with the senses as well as with the spirit; it requires factual happenings, apparently pure contingencies in time; it requires a central affirmation of a Reality other and deeper than the single soul, however rich, than Humanity, however complete, than the totality of all finite intelligences and lives, however superior to man.

EA 2, p. 124

Such science will help to discipline, humble, purify the natural eagerness and wilfulness, the cruder forms of anthropomorphism, of the human mind and heart. This turning to the visible will thus largely take the place of that former turning away from it; for only since the Visible has been taken to represent laws, and, provisionally at least, rigorously mechanical laws characteristic of itself, can it be thus looked upon as a means of spiritual purification.

Such science again will help to stimulate those other, deeper activities of human nature, which have made possible, and have all along preceded and accompanied, these more superficial ones; and this, although such science will doubtless tend to do the very opposite, if the whole nature be allowed to become exclusively engrossed in this one phenomenal direction. Still it remains true that perhaps never has man turned to the living God more happily and humbly, than when coming straight away from such rigorous, disinterested phenomenal analysis, as long as such analysis is felt to be both other than, preliminary and secondary to, the deepest depths of the soul's life and of all ultimate Reality.

And finally, such science will correspondingly help to give depth and mystery, drama and pathos, a rich spirituality, to the whole experience and conception of the soul and of life, of the world and of God. Instead of a more or less abstract picture, where all is much on the same plane, where all is either fixed and frozen, or all is in a state of feverish flux, we get an outlook,

with foreground, middle distances, and background, each con-
trasting with, each partially obscuring, partially revealing, the
other; but each doing so, with any freshness and fullness, only
in and through the strongly willing, the fully active and gladly
suffering, the praying, aspiring, and energizing spiritual Personality, which thus both gives and gets its own true self ever more
entirely and more deeply.

ME 1, pp. 44-45

But just as the institutional easily tends to a weakening both
of the Intellectual and of the Emotional, so does the Emotional
readily turn against not only the Institutional but against the
Intellectual as well. This latter hostility will take two forms.
Inasmuch as the feeling clings to historical facts and persons,
it will instinctively elude or attempt to suppress all critical
examination and analysis of these its supports. Inasmuch as it
feeds upon its own emotion, which (as so much pure emotion)
is, at any one of its stages, ever intensely one and intensely exclusive, it will instinctively fret under and oppose all that slow
discrimination and mere approximation, that collection of a few
certainties, many probabilities, and innumerable possibilities, all
that pother over a very little, which seem to make up the sum
of all human knowledge. Such Emotion will thus tend to be
hostile to Historical Criticism, and to all the Critical, Analytic
stages and forms of Philosophy. It turns away instinctively from
the cold manifold of thinking; and it shrinks spontaneously from
the hard opaque of action and of the external. All this will again
be found to be borne out by history.

A combination of Institutionalism and Experimentalism against
Intellectualism is another not infrequent abuse, and one which
is not hard to explain. For if external, definite facts and acts are
found to lead to certain internal, deep, all-embracing emotions and
experiences, the soul can to a certain extent live and thrive in and
by a constant moving backwards and forwards between the Institution and the Emotion alone, and can thus constitute an
ever-tightening bond and dialogue, increasingly exclusive of all
else. For although the Institution will, taken in itself, retain for
the Emotion a certain dryness and hardness, yet the Emotion
can and often does associate with this Institution whatever that
contact with it has been found to bring and to produce. And if
the Institution feels hard and obscure, it is not, like the Thinking, cold and transparent. Just because the Institution appears

to the emotional nature as though further from its feeling, and yet is experienced as a mysterious cause or occasion of this feeling, the emotional nature is fairly, often passionately, ready to welcome what it can thus rest on and lean on as something having a comfortable fixity both of relation and of resistance. But with regard to Thinking, all this is different. For thought is sufficiently near to Feeling, necessarily to produce friction and competition of some sort, and seems, with its keen edge and endless mobility, to be the born implacable foe of the dull, dead givenness of any one Emotional mood.

ME, 1, pp. 75–76

But, is not such a (frictional) view of life Epicurean? Where is the Cross and Self-Renunciation? Is it not Christ Himself who has bidden us cut off our right hand and pluck out our right eye, if they offend; who has declared that he who hateth not his own father and mother for His sake is not worthy of Him; who has asked, 'What doth it profit a man, if he gain the whole world, and suffer the loss of his own soul?' and who has pronounced a special woe upon the rich, and a special blessing upon the poor in spirit? Does not our view, on the contrary, bid a man attend to his hands and eyes, rather than to their possible or even actual offending, euphemistically described here as 'friction'; bid him love his father and mother, even though this introduce a conflict into his affections; bid him take care to gain, as far as may be, the whole of his own possible interior and exterior world, as though this would of itself be equivalent to his saving his soul; and thus bid him become rich and full and complex, an aesthete rather than a man of God? In a word, is not our position a masked Paganism, a new Renaissance rather than the noble Christianity?

Now here again a true answer is found in a clear intelligence of the actual implications of the position. For if the Intellectual action were here taken as capable of alone, or in any degree directly, forming the foundation of all our other life, so that on a mathematically clear and complete system, appealing to and requiring the abstractive powers alone, would, later on, be built, according to our own further determination, the Institutional and Experimental, or both or neither; then such a position, if possible and actualized, would indeed save us the simultaneous energizing of our whole complex nature, and would, so far, well deserve the accusation of unduly facilitating life; it might be taken as, at least, not beginning with the Cross. But here this is not so. For from the first the External and the Mystical elements are held to be at least as necessary and operative as the Intellectual element; and it is impossible to see how the elimination of this latter, and of the ever-expensive keeping it and its rivals each at their own work, could deepen the truly moral sufferings and sacrifices of the soul's life.

If again the Intellectual action were taken, as by Gnosticism of all sorts, as the eventual goal of the whole, so that the External and Mystical would end by being absorbed into the Intellectual, our Knowledge becoming coextensive with Reality itself, then we might again, and with still deeper truth, be accused of eliminating the element of effort and of sacrifice,—the Cross. But here, on the contrary, not only the Intellectual alone does not conclude and crown it. Eternally will different soul-functions conjoin in a common work, eternally will God and the souls of our fellows be for us realities in diverse degrees outside of and beyond our own apprehension of them, and eternally shall we apprehend them differently and to a different degree by our intelligence, by our affection, and by our volition. Hence, even in eternity itself we can, without exceeding the limits of sober thinking and of psychological probability, find a field for the exercise by our souls of something corresponding to the joy and greatness of noble self-sacrifice here below. The loving soul will there, in the very home of love, give itself wholly to and be fulfilled by God, and yet the soul will possess an indefinitely heightened apprehension of the immense excess of this its love and act above its knowledge, and of God Himself above both. And here again it is impossible to see how the elimination of the intellectual element, which becomes thus the very measure of the soul's own limitations, and of the exceeding greatness of its love and of its Lover, would make the conception more efficaciously humbling and Christian.

Both at the beginning, then, and throughout, and even at the end of the soul's life, the intellectual element is necessary, and this above all for the planting fully and finally, in the very depths of the personality, the Cross, the sole means to the soul's true Incoronation.

ME 1, pp. 81–82

For one thing, this gigantic Social Problem brings home, even to the sleepy traditionalist or recalcitrant official, with demonstrative clearness and clamorous intensity, how large is the dependence of the growth and power of the religious experiences and requirements, amongst average human beings, upon a certain security and stability in the means and circumstances of physical existence, and especially upon some family life and leisure. The cases of the Galilean 'poor', i.e., small fishermen and husbandmen, whom Our Lord declared to be blessed, or, again, the Umbrian peasantry and workmen addressed by the *Poverello* of Assisi in his homely open-air discourses, are here nowise in point. The problem is not simply intensified for us, it is radically changed; and this change has made us realise, more clearly than ever before, the great dependence of the chances and articulation of religion upon the various social conditions of the average human beings addressed by it. This we now see to apply even to the Primitive Christian and Mediaeval world and religion, and it is doubly applicable to our present conditions.

This indeed is the element of profound truth parodied, because taken as complete, by the Socialists, and almost as keenly, but more wisely, apprehended by the various Christian Social workers. For the latter, with whatever excesses or even errors, all strongly realise the necessity, for the average man, of some social and sanitary roominess and decency, of some home life, some assurance concerning the morrow, and some little leisure, as preliminaries for the growth within him of the religious instincts and of an echo to religious appeals.

EL, pp. 314–315

We found the dispositions necessary for the unhampered spreading throughout the whole of life of the soundness resident in the deepest roots—in Superhuman Religion, to be three : the soberly autonomous development of the several non-religious faculties and of the non-religious associations of man; the ready recognition, by any one religion, of elements of worth variously present in the other religions, together with the careful avoidance of all attempts at forced conformity; and a careful respect for the methods intrinsic to history and philosophy, even where these analyse or theorise the documents and experiences of religion itself. Thus will all men of good faith be laid open to the appeal, so full of aid to the best that is in them, of Superhuman Religion in its profound life and reality.

EA. p. 66

Chapter VII

PHILOSOPHY AND RELIGION:
MAN'S PLUMB-LINE AND GOD'S REALITY

V ON HÜGEL knew the human mind too well to assume that it
could get on by ignoring or rejecting some kind of a philosophical map that would relate its religious experience to
experience in other areas. He knew the vulnerability of an anti-
intellectualist religion to the current charges that all religion is at
bottom a mental creation, a mere projection of the mind, in short,
an illusion.

He warmly commended some species of realism where the object
we apprehend retains its 'givenness', its priority, its independence,
its ultimate initiative; and where the subject—our knowing mind—
for all of its contribution to the act of knowing, is kept humble, and
seeking, and open: is kept as the discoverer and not the creator of
what comes to it.

He believed that only in a climate of some such form of realism
could both the integrity and the relative autonomies, on the one
hand, and yet the creative friction between the spiritual experience
of God, the physical world which science articulates for us, and the
witness of art and moral striving, on the other hand, be vindicated
and each be secured from some cheap reductionism into terms of
the other that would sell one or another of them short.

Within this climate of realism, von Hügel was convinced that
both religion and science could freely admit that their formulations
of their prime object of concern might be subject to reconstitution
without in any way denying the reality of their object. And within
realism, both science and religion might admit how a final beyond
always managed to elude the exhaustiveness of their formulations
although it did not necessarily falsify them.

He opens what were to have been his Gifford lectures on *The
Reality of God* with the following statement:

Introduction

How strange is the well-known law, so often forgotten, that what comes first in reality and existence comes last in our apprehension and clear grasp! Over fifty years have been given by me to the practice and to the analysis and theory of religion, and yet it is only within the last few years that I have attained to anything like clearness concerning the roots of such faith, and such knowledge, as I now have, of such faith, whether achieved or given or both, as I have possessed from the first or successively or have come to hold by both processes. For how long time, for instance, I *would* try to find the most adequate formulation of these deepest things in a more or less Idealistic philosophy of an Hegelian type, assumed to be baptizable and indeed baptized. By 'Idealist' I mean any philosophy which is so full of the undoubted activities of the subject as largely to overlook the distinct reality and the influence of the object. Yet all along I can now see well, as I look back, my mind was never really comfortable in these, at bottom, fantastic curtailments of what we really do and achieve, of what is really given to us every time we know, and indeed think, at all: the essential, the inevitable *transcendence* present in all our knowledge, so that knowledge is never primarily simply a knowledge of our states, but a knowledge, or at least the seeking for a knowledge, of the objects which exist prior to, and after each and every attempt on the part of myself or of all such to apprehend and to articulate.

After all, it is a sheer fact that some kind of Realism is in possession.

RG. p. 3

Metaphysics, Ontology, to this degree at least, are thus of the very essence of religion; religion is, primarily, a need, an experience, and an affirmation of what is; and only in the second instance a command as to what ought to be. Because our Father *is*, and because the blessed *are* and do His will in heaven: because of this (and not because the time is short or long before we have to leave this lower scene) are we to do this same Divine Will, as nearly as we can, here upon our earth.

GS, p. 39

Astronomy and Geology have been busy from the first not with fancies but with realities, and these realities cannot, for themselves, be other than this or that, and not this *and* that:

true, but the human minds that peer out at these realities can and do, indeed, apprehend these realities largely, after all, as they are in themselves, and yet with certain incompletenesses and imperfections which only they could remove. These several removals do not alter the object perceived, the object remains in itself precisely what it was from the very first, nor do men lose faith in human reason : they only experience the very simple fact that it is an instrument requiring adaptation and readaptation to the object of which it is in search.

RG, p. 147

In my own case it was Geology which made the notion that the human mind creates reality a preposterous one. Already at eighteen I cared much for Devonian and Cretaceous rocks and their contents of plants and animals. Recently I have come back to my geology, and, instead of Lyell, I have studied Archibald Geikie—and what do I find?Well, those favourite formations of mine of fifty years before have been studied on a far larger scale and in much greater detail, and many so great minds have been engrossed on that rich subject-matter throughout the intervening half-century that at first I have some difficulty in finding my way about in what had been so familiar to me; but—and what a joy this was!—that Devonian and this Cretaceous period were there, unmistakably and substantially, as they had been half a century before. Only these subject-matters were now known with a greater articulation; fresh problems had arisen in place of the old, when those older subject-matters had been more or less definitely answered; and so I was not simply face to face with the interesting, or for the most part very uninteresting, history of my own mind, but with facts of immense length and range in space and time, distinct from my little self, yet part of that great which has environed me from the first moment of my existence, and which from the first has awakened me to a sense of its reality and the corresponding consciousness of myself; facts loved by me precisely in their distinctness. A sceptical German philosopher of the greatest distinction as a philosopher commentator wrote that, after all, it did not really much matter, at least as regards our enjoyment, whether religion were or were not just simply the projection of our minds; since there would always remain the pleasure of our being able to produce such constructions. How strangely unperceptive! Why, not only religion but geology, but astronomy, depend for our enjoyment of them primarily upon our sense, upon our feeling, of the real distinction of the real objects from ourselves and yet of our genuine apprehension of them! Try and prove, if you will, that religion is untrue; but do not mislead yourself and others as to what constitutes its power and its worth.

RG, pp. 4–5

Man's religious apprehensions and conceptions will ever necessarily be mixed up with considerable inadequacy, mostly even of the avoidable kind and with much evil passion and positive error; hence at the later stages he considers the earlier stages are full of, sometimes as sheer, delusion. And these developments have, so far, moved, chiefly, away from external nature to the inner life of man. Yet also the much easier, because less deep, physical sciences have admittedly maintained, for millenniums, the most far-reaching, most fantastic errors, so that they readily appear, if we insist on this fact, as sheer, incorrigible illusions, nevertheless we rightly maintain them, as increasingly true and as possessed, from the first, of some real connection with Reality. And much points to man's again finding, in the future, and then with indefinite increase of precision, the Spirit at work in the visible world. Unless the Irishman's argument was sound that, because a certain stove would save him half his fuel, two such stoves would save it all, there is no necessary consequence, from the admission of such an admixture of illusion with truth, to the negation of the operative presence of some reality within this long series of human apprehensions.

EL, pp. 238–239

. . . Not all the childishness, abuses, trials, variously attributable to the different religions of the world, can permanently obscure the magnificent, indeed unique, services of religion. How can we retain Plato and Leibnitz, Phidias and Michaelangelo, Homer and Shakespeare in highest honour, as revealers of various degrees and kinds of reality and truth, if Amos and Isaiah, Paul and Augustine, Francis of Assisi and Joan of Arc are to be treated as pure illusionists, in precisely that which constitutes their specific power and attestation?

EL, pp. 240–241

And it is the action of all that objective, variously inter-related world upon this human subject, itself a world within that world, and this human subject's response (from his senses up to his reason, feeling, will) to that world's action, which is primary; whereas the abstracting activity is secondary and instrumental, and necessarily never fully overtakes those primary informations. The more real the subject stimulated and reacting, and the more real the object stimulating and acting, the more 'inside' does each possess, and the more rich, and the more difficult clearly to analyse, will be the result of such stimulus and response.

EL, p. 237

The deeper we get into reality, the more numerous will be the questions we cannot answer. For myself I cannot conceive truth, or rather reality, as a geometrical figure of luminous lines, within which is sheer truth, and outside of which is sheer error; but I have to conceive such reality as light, in its centre blindingly luminous, having rings around it of lesser and lesser light, growing dimmer and dimmer until we are left in utter darkness. I cannot answer the endless questions naturally provoked by my positions; but this incapacity need not prove more than that I am a finite mind, and that, although other finite minds can and will correct its weaknesses and errors, and although the realm of light can and will be indefinitely enlarged, yet its borders will continue fringed—they will never be clear-cut frontiers. For reality is more than any and all our imaginings of it. It is more than truth; it overwhelms whilst it supports us; and it will have produced one of its chief functions and effects if it keeps us thoroughly humbled in its presence—from the presence of the daisy to the presence and reality of God.

RG, p. 33

In such a conception of the place of Science, we have permanently to take Science, throughout life, in a double sense and way. In the first instance, Science is self-sufficing, its own end and its own law. In the second instance, which alone is ever final, Science is but a part of a whole, but a function, a necessary yet preliminary function, of the whole of man; and it is but a part, a necessary yet preliminary part, of his outlook. Crush out, or in any way mutilate or de-autonomise, this part, and all the rest will suffer. Sacrifice the rest to this part, either by starvation or attempted suppression, or by an impatient assimilation of this immense remainder to that smaller and more superficial part, and the whole man suffers again, and much more seriously.

And the danger, in both directions,—let us have the frankness to admit the fact,—is constant and profound : even to see it continuously is difficult; to guard against it with effect, most difficult indeed. For to starve or to suspect, to cramp or to crush this phenomenal apprehension and investigation, in the supposed interest of the ulterior truths, must ever be a besetting temptation and weakness for the religious instinct, wherever this instinct is strong and fixed, and has not yet itself been put in the way of purification.

For Religion is ever, *qua* religion, authoritative and absolute. What constitutes religion is not simply to hold a view and to try to live a life, with respect to the Unseen and the Deity, as possibly or even certainly beautiful or true or good : but precisely that which is over and above this, the holding this view and this life to proceed somehow from God Himself, so as to bind my innermost mind and conscience to unhesitating assent. Not simply that I think it, but that, in addition, I feel bound to think it, transforms a thought about God into a religious act.

Now this at once brings with it a double and most difficult problem. For Religion thus becomes, by its very genius and in exact proportion to its reality, something so entirely *sui generis*, so claimful and supreme, that it at once exacts a two-fold submission, the one simultaneous, the other successive; the first as it were in space, the second in time. The first regards the relations of religion to things non-religious. It might be parodied by saying : 'Since religion is true and supreme, religion is all we require : all things else must be bent or broken to her sway.' She has at the very least the right to primacy not of honour only, but of direct jurisdiction, over and within all activities and things. The second regards the form and concept of religion itself. Since religion always appears both in a particular form at a particular time and place, *and* as divine and hence authoritative and eternal; and since the very strength and passion of religion depend upon the vigorous presence and close union of these two elements : religion will ever tend either really to oppose all change within itself, or else to explain away its existence. Religion would thus appear doomed to be either vague and inoperative, or obscurantist and insincere.

And it is equally clear that the other parts of man's nature and of his outlook cannot simply accept such a claim, nor could religion itself flourish at all if they could and did accept it. They cannot accept the claim of religion to be immediately and simply all, for they are fully aware of being themselves something also. They cannot accept her claim to dictate to them their own domestic laws, for they are fully aware that they each, to live truly at all, require their own laws and their own, at least relative, autonomy. However much man may be supremely and finally a religious animal, he is not *only* that; but he is a physical and sexual, a fighting and an artistic, a domestic and social, a political and philosophical animal as well.

Nor can man, even simply *qua* religious man, consent to a simple finality in the experience and explication, in the apprehension and application of religion, either in looking back into the past; or in believing and loving, suffering and acting in the present; or in forecasting the future, either of the race or of himself alone. For the *here and now*, the concrete 'immediacy', the unique individuality of the religious experience for *me*, in this room, on this very day, its freshness, is as true and necessary a quality of living religion as any other whatsoever. And if all life sustains itself only by constant, costing renovation and adaptation of itself to its environment, the religious life, as the most intense and extensive of all lives, must somehow be richest in such newness in oldness, such renovative, adaptive, assimilative power.

Now it is deeply instructive to observe all this at work historically. For here we find every variety of attitude towards this very point. There are men of Religion who attempt to do without Science, and men of Science who attempt to do without Religion. Or again, men of Religion attempt to *level up*,—to assimilate the principles and results of the various sciences directly to religion, or at least to rule those scientific principles and results directly by religion. Or men of Science attempt to *level down*, to make religion into a mere philosophy or even a natural history. Yet we find also,—with so persistent a recurrence in all manner of places and times, as itself to suggest the inherent, essential, indestructible truth of the view,—another, a far more costing attitude. This attitude refuses all mutilation whether of normal human nature or of its outlook, all oppression of one part by the other; for it discovers that these various levels of life have been actually practised in conjunction by many an individual in the past and in the present.

ME 1, pp. 45-47

Von Hügel is quite clear that philosophy, while it is indispensable to a religious life that is to grow and expand its horizons, must not usurp the function of religion and pretend that it can replace it and that religion is only an earlier kindergarten, a premetaphysical stage to be outgrown. He also has a haunting sense that transcendence marks all deeply held experience whether it be that of a Buddhist who feels the unreality of sense experience, or of a scientific researcher who knows what a frail and ephemeral shell his formulation of the physical world really is, or an artist who senses that the goal has escaped him in the best thing he ever produced, or a moral man who knows how far he still is from perfect love, or a religious man who knows how fragile is his symbol of the living God that seeks to express that blindingly real presence that has swept and changed him.

Now what especially Hume here fails utterly to see, is the dependence of philosophy, for its materials and experiences, indirectly also for its estimates and graduations of religion, upon the historical and social religions, upon the various cults and Churches. Any one, all of these complexes may demand criticism, checks, completion from other levels and activities of man— especially also from philosophy; philosophy may be a useful, possibly an irreplaceable aid in more and more completely arriving at what in the religions is most specifically religious, and how and where they should stand in a classification of them. But philosophy no more makes religion than botany makes plants or astronomy suns and moons; and criticism of all sorts is—in these deep matters especially—worse than useless unless it is inspired by a genuine experience and love of religion. Hence we must here always have our nails before we pare them; we must pare them, not in order to make them or to have them, but in order to keep them in as nearly as possible the size, shape and other conditions in which, from long and manifold experience, we find nails ought to be.

Thus love—love of religion, and love of the other kinds, levels, ranges of life—is here the fundamental need—a standing within these living complexes and necessities. The concrete has here always to come first, and to be reached last; the criticism, the aloofness, the negation has everywhere to remain a means, not the end, a pain, not a pleasure.

EA 2, pp. 130–131

And finally, life, after all, at its deepest, is a stretching out of faith and love to God into the dark. Philosophy ends, surely, with certain *desiderata* and possibilities, which religion meets, exceeds, traverses, restates; and religion is a circle of experience, possessed of its own character, contents, and conditions, which, as man's first and last and deepest experience, will indeed greatly exceed philosophy in richness but fall short of it in direct clearness and detailed articulation. Whereas these writers, *qua* Hegelians, give us, in and through philosophy, already the substance of what we get in religion; both these variants of the final light and word here are (seeing we are dealing with finite man's ultimate apprehensions of the Infinite) astonishingly clear and complete; and indeed, clearness and completeness being here the dominant, determining, character, philosophy cannot escape from being held the 'truer', because the clearer and completer, form of outlook. And yet how can philosophy, or such a philosophy, be man's ultimate faith, an outlook that ignores or minimizes temptation, doubt, sin; that knows so little of the homeliness alone truly appropriate to man, the created and the weak; that is not centrally love seeking and finding Love in trial and in darkness? Gethsemane and Calvary, are they truly, fully here?

EL, pp. 222–223

I believe, then, that religion, at its deepest and in the long run, is not and never will be satisfied short of pressing on to, short of intimations from, the really Ultimate. It will persist as a conviction in the real, present existence of the Absolute, intimating this Its existence in the necessary implications of our thought, emotions and action, and in our most incurable dissatisfactions in Aesthetics, Ethics, Metaphysics.

EA 2, p. 205

... We are here (in Buddhism) given perhaps the most impressive of all exemplifications of the intolerable horror felt, by the wide-awake human soul, for mere succession of any kind. The pain of such sheer flux, already simply because it *is* sheer flux, is here seen to be such that the soul, which is haunted by the image and sense of such a flux, is too much absorbed in the relief afforded by any and every complete escape from his pain to move on towards the apprehension of full spiritual life,—of *duration*, and of perfect *Simultaneity*, as respectively the ceaseless characteristic and the deepest implication of that life. And yet that horror eloquently expresses this very characteristic and this very implication of the human soul's deeper and deepest life.

EL, p. 10

Some years ago alarm grew rife concerning the safety of Winchester Cathedral, discovered to be undermined by water-courses; and expert divers, in full diving dress, plunged down through the springs to the swamps and sands—the foundations so daringly accepted by the original builders of the majestic edifice. The divers found the great oaken beams, as laid by those first builders upon those shifting natural foundations still, for the most part, serviceably sound. Yet some of these beams required replacing; and the guardian architects decided to replace them all by great concrete piers. We, too, in this study, have been probing foundations—those of Religion. But here we have found the foundations to consist of rock—two interdependent, interclamped rock-masses: the general, dim and dumb Religiosity—the more or less slumbering sense and need of the Abiding and Eternal; and the concrete, precise and personal Religion—the clear answer to that confused asking, and, with this answer, the now keen articulation of that dim demand. And both that general dull sense and this special definite presentment were found by us in actual life,—found by us there as Givennesses of an evidential, revelational, an other-than-human, a more-than-human quality.

EA, pp. 65–66

Chapter VIII

IMMORTALITY, SUFFERING, THE ROLE OF JESUS CHRIST AND HEROIC WITNESS

O N the subject of immortality, the Baron puts the accent on God and on its beginning here in this life. On evil, he is humble and proffers no facile explanation but only an example of how it was overcome by Jesus Christ and how Christians are called out to transform it. These counsels point to the work of Jesus Christ at the heart of things and with the called-outness of supernatural action on the part of ordinary men and women in the midst of a life where evil and suffering are everywhere. Von Hügel once quoted Huvelin as saying, 'I am allergic to miracles'. His own position is never one of denying miracles in general or the Biblical miracles in particular, but 'the spiritual life of prayer, of Love, and of Devotedness is even in its fullest Christian developments essentially not miraculous but supernatural' (*EA*, p. 279). And it was in this supernatural witness all through the fabric of life that von Hügel found a major religious *fact* that pointed beyond itself, to the one who draws all men to himself.

The simple fact, assuredly, is that the soul, *qua* religious, has no interest in just simple unending existence, of no matter what kind or of a merely natural kind—an existence with God at most as the dim background to a vivid experience of its own unending natural existence. The specifically religious desire of Immortality begins, not with Immortality, but with God; it rests upon God; and it ends in God. The religious soul does not seek, find, or assume its own Immortality; and thereupon seek, find, or assume God. But it seeks, finds, experiences, and loves God; and because of God, and of this, its very real though still very imperfect, intercourse with God—because of these experiences which lie right within the noblest joy, fears, hopes, necessities, certainties which emerge within any and every field of its life here below—it finds, rather than seeks, Immortality of a certain kind. The very slow but solidly sure, the very sober but severely spiritual, growth of the belief in Immortality amongst the Jews, a belief fully endorsed and greatly developed by our Lord, was entirely thus—not from Immortality of no matter what kind to God, but from God to a special kind of Immortality. Especially does Christ always keep God and the Kingdom of God central, as the beginning and end of all, and the Immortality peripheral, as but the extension and full establishment of the soul's supernatural union with, and of its supernatural activity towards, God and man.

EA, p. 197

There is here a lively conviction that our spiritual personality, and its full beatitude, can never be attained in this life, but only in the other life after death; and yet that the other life can begin in this life, indeed that we are, all of us, more or less solicited, here and now, by that other life, and that we cannot consummate it *there*, unless we begin it *here*.

EL, p. 367

I will but add that, in proportion as we move up in the scale of reality, the more we have to conceive the Divine Action as bafflingly rich and varied in the manner, the degree, and the restraint of its operation and aid; and that, in proportion as we insist upon God's Immanence within the sensible and human world, in the same proportion does the problem of Evil increase in urgency and difficulty. Yet both these mysteries appear to be intrinsic to life, and religion, which has not caused or imagined them, can bear them; indeed only religion can, if not theoretically explain, at least practically utilize and surmount the wondrous and dread capabilities and realities thus experienced by us in our lives and in the world.

EL, pp. 287–288

I do not see, I have never seen, why any man should be called upon to answer everything, or why a position may not be profoundly true though it involves at once difficulties beyond solution by the wit of man. Not only do we see here in a glass darkly, but often and at many points we do not see at all; would it not be better simply to admit this where it is really necessary, and nevertheless, go on insisting upon our light where it is light?

RG, p. 124

No, let us quietly and deliberately admit that no man has yet explained the reality of evil—I mean, of course, the fact of genuine evil, especially moral evil, in a world created and sustained by an all-powerful, all-wise, all-good Spirit, by God.

My second, not refutation but quieting consideration, springs from the way in which Judaism first a little and then Christianity considerably more has, not intellectually explained how evil can exist, but has somehow made men capable of bearing and transfiguring this evil. Here I do not doubt that we are on the safest ground. We dare not urge even this point as something of mathematical, demonstrable power, since I have known myself and you, reader, have doubtless known also cases where much suffering had thoroughly soured the soul, and this, as far as one could judge, without any serious fault on the part of the poor soul thus soured. Yet this does not prevent the reality of those cases where the nettle has been grasped and where evil has in itself remained evil, where suffering and trouble of all sorts have never ceased to be recognized as things evil in themselves, but where somehow they really have become, not of course mechanical, necessary causes of transformation, but the occasion, the partial means of such change.

Christianity stands towards the problem of evil very certainly in a uniquely satisfactory way; for it is Christianity which has undoubtedly most deepened and widened our sense of the reality of evil and of the special repulsiveness of moral evil, and, on the other hand, it is Christianity alone, literally alone, which has known what to do with suffering, with suffering, I mean, as a concrete fact in the lives of us all and which, quite apart from any satisfactory explanation, we have to locate in our several existences to prevent its crushing us, and to succeed, if at all possible, in turning it into the occasion of virtues undreamt of or, at least, quite unexercised before. And it is precisely in this practical grappling with suffering, in its utilization and acceptance as an intrument for the widening, deepening, and purifying of the soul, that Christianity has achieved truly amazing results; and there is nothing to show that, though men be civilized and educated and washed and physicked by the State as much as is ever remotely conceivable, there would not be suffering and apparently an increase of suffering, at least in the mental and spiritual regions of man's many-levelled life.

RG, pp. 17–18

For Christianity, without ever a hesitation, from the first and everywhere, refused to hold, or even to tolerate, either the one or the other of the two only attempts at self-persuasion which, then as now, possess souls that suffer whilst they have not yet found the deepest. Christianity refused all Epicureanism,—since man cannot find his deepest by fleeing from pain and suffering, and by seeking pleasure and pleasures, however dainty and refined. And it refused all Stoicism,—since pain, suffering, evil are not fancies and prejudices, but real, very real; and since man's greatest action and disposition is not self-sufficingness or aloofness, but self-donation and love. Christianity refused these theories, not by means of another theory of its own, but simply by exhibiting a Life and lives—the Life of the Crucified, and lives which continually re-live, in their endless various lesser degrees and ways, such a combination of gain in giving and of joy in suffering. Christianity thus gave to souls the faith and strength to grasp life's nettle. It raised them, in their deepest dispositions and innermost will, above the pitiful oscillations and artificialities of even the greatest of the Pagans in this central matter,—between eluding, ignoring pain and suffering, and, animal-like, seeking life in its fleeting, momentary pleasures; or trying the nobler yet impossible course,—the making out that physical, mental, moral pain and evil are nothing real, and the suppressing of emotion, sympathy and pity as things unworthy of the adult soul. Christianity did neither. It pointed to Jesus with the terror of death upon Him in Gethsemane; with a cry of desolation upon the Cross on Cavalry; it allowed the soul, it encouraged the soul to sob itself out. It not only taught men frankly to face and to recognise physical and mental pain, death, and all other, especially all moral evils and sufferings as very real; it actually showed men the presence and gravity of a host of pains, evils and miseries which they had, up to then, quite ignored or at least greatly minimised. And yet, with all this—in spite of all such material for despair, the final note of Christianity was and is still, one of trust, of love, of transcendent joy. It is no accident, but of the very essence of the mystery and of the power of faith, it springs from the reality of God and of His action within men's souls, that, as the nobly joyous last chapters of Isaiah (Chap. 40 to the end) contain also those wondrous utterances of the man of sorrows, so also the serenity of the Mount of the Beatitudes leads, in the Gospels, to the darkness of Calvary.

Pray believe me here: it is to Christianity that we owe our deepest insight into the wondrously wide and varied range throughout the world, as we know it, of pain, suffering, evil; just as to Christianity we owe the richest enforcement of the fact that, in spite of all this, God *is*, and that He is good and loving. And this enforcement Christianity achieves, at its best, by actually inspiring soul after soul, to believe, to love, to live this wondrous faith.

EA, pp. 111–113

The very certain fact is that Evil — physical, mental, moral—is real, is prevalent, is apparently triumphant—at least throughout wide areas and long periods of life. No theory has ever explained it; no attempt at its evaporation by means of some Neo-Platonist discovery that it is essentially only negative—the absence, or the lesser presence, of good: no such tricks and evasions could fail most rightly to irritate through and through so sincere, and mostly so unsophisticated, a mind as was that of Lyell. Here again, if this be Agnosticism, we ought all to be agnostics. Indeed, here again, we all, in our better moments, are such agnostics; the explaining away of evil as non-real, or even as in itself a good, will always remain ineffective, even for the explainers themselves—provided they fortunately retain their human normality and sensitiveness—in times of lonely suffering and interior defeat.

Certainly Christianity, at its best, has not attempted such unreal and presumptuous explanations or denials. It has done two very different, much greater, things. Christianity has indefinitely deepened our perception of evil, in making us note the most poignant sufferings in precisely the most God-united souls, and, still more, in making us see and admit the worst evil in the possibility, in the actual existence, of the voluntary perversion of the will and character, as furnished by more or less deliberate sin. And Christianity has thereupon, not theoretically explained this problem, thus greatly deepened by itself, but it has practically overcome it in its various actual manifestations. Our Lord's agony of fear and of desolation in Gethsemane and on the Cross become the very instruments, occasions, and expressions of the fullest, tenderest love of God and by God; and a Magdalene and an Augustine stand forth, as penitent saints, as true moral miracles of spiritual re-creation.

RG, p. 183

His (Jesus's) teaching, His life, are all positive, all constructive, and come into conflict only with worldly indifference and bad faith. No teacher before Him or since, but requires, if we would not be led astray by him, that we should make some allowances, in his character and doctrine, for certain inevitable reactions, and consequent narrowness and contrarinesses. Especially is this true of religious teachers and reformers, and generally in exact proportion to the intensity of their fervour. But in Him there is no reaction, no negation, no fierceness, of a kind to deflect His teaching from its immanent, self-consistent trend. His very Apostles can ask Him to call down fire from Heaven upon the unbelieving Samaritans; they can use the sword against one of those come out to apprehend Him; and they can attempt to keep the little ones from Him. But He rebukes them; He orders Peter to put back the sword in its scabbard; and He bids the little ones to come unto Him, since of such is the Kingdom of Heaven. Indeed St Mark's Gospel tells us how the disciples begged Him to forbid a man who did not follow them from casting out devils in His name; and how He refused to do so, and laid down the great universal rule of all-embracing generosity : 'He that is not against us, is for us.'

ME 1, pp. 27–28

It is in the Synoptics that we get . . . the most spontaneous and many sided expression of that divinely human, widely traditional and social, and welcoming and all-transforming spirit.

ME 2, pp. 118–119

In any case, the writer could not, in a serious study of Eternal Life, pass over this, the deepest and most operative revelation concerning the Temporal and the Eternal ever vouchsafed to man. And here he would take his stand very deliberately with those who indeed find a genuine and full eschatological element in Our Lord's life and teaching, yet who discover it there as but one of two movements or elements—a gradual, prophetic, immanental, predominantly ethical element; and this sudden, apocalyptic, transcendental, purely religious element. Indeed, the interaction, the tension, between these two elements or movements, is ultimately found to be an essential constituent, and part of the mainspring, of Christianity, of religion, and (in some form) even of all the deepest spiritual life.

It is, surely, very interesting to note how that brilliant German-French teacher and writer, Albert Schweitzer . . . has found even this (Apocalyptic) picture of Christ so deeply fascinating for his own soul, that he has abandoned his high posts and brilliant prospects in Europe, and has gone, (to Africa) as a simple medical missionary.

EL, pp. viii-ix

We find, then, that the first Apostles, and even still—predominantly—St. Paul also, really believed that Our Lord would promptly, during the lifetime of some of them, appear again upon earth, and make all human conditions radically new; and we find that, in Our Lord's own teaching also, the shortness of the persistence of our visible world's present order is implied, taught, solemnly insisted upon. His Proximate Second Coming, with its profound change and conclusion of all earthly conditions, becomes especially emphasised from the great scene with Peter at Caesarea Philippi onwards. Even if we could explain away certain central affirmations of the utmost solemnity and clearness, there would still remain all those generous, most authentic parables, from after that scene, which so markedly insist upon the abrupt, proximate, purely God-given end and renovation of all things in His Second Coming, and upon, on our own part, utter detachment and strenuous watchfulness. These parables of storm, stress, suddenness and transcendence, are certainly authentic, but not more so than are the parables of the first joyous, expansive period, which emphasise the slow growth, the successive development, the immanent ethical work and enjoyment of the soul upon and within itself, in this beautiful world of physical sunshine, air, wind and rain, flowers, birds and children.

It is clear that we can either concentrate upon the relatively immanent, ethical, continuous, out-going, joyous movement, or upon the exclusively transcendent, religious, abrupt, incoming, heroic movement, or upon both. And only the last concentration —the fructifying, alternating of one movement by and with the other—gives us the complete Jesus, the true genius of Christianity. And thus we get this genius to consist, essentially, not in a list of things absolutely wrong, and in another list of things absolutely right—but, even more than in a small list of things always and simply wrong, in the continuous sense that the very things we, men, are to love and seek are also the same things which we are to be detached from, and from which we are to flee. Attachment and cultivation, and detachment and renouncement will thus each gain and keep a splendid spaciousness of occasions and materials. There will be no fanaticism, but a profound earnestness; there will be no worldliness, but an immense variety of interest and expansion towards all things in their specific kinds and degrees of goodness, truth and beauty.

EA, 2, pp. 81–82

In the Italian Alps I used to love a certain deep, ever sunless gorge, through which a resounding mountain torrent was continuously fighting its way, without rest, without fruit. Why did I love it so? Doubtless because I realised, amidst that sterile-seeming uproar, that, down far away, this torrent would spread itself out as a sunlit, peaceful, fertilizing river, slowly flowing through the rich plains of Piedmont. So it is with the Apocalyptic Jesus and with the Prophetic Jesus, indeed with both these Jesuses and the ever-present Christ.

EA, p. 142

Thus the very same act and reasons which completely bind me, do so only to true growth and to indefinite expansion. I shall, it is true, ever go back and cling to the definite spatial and temporal manifestations of this infinite Spirit's personality, but I shall, by this same act, proclaim His eternal presentness and inexhaustible self-interpreting illumination. By the same act by which I believe in the revelation of the workshop of Nazareth, of the Lake of Galilee, of Gethesemane and Calvary, I believe that this revelation is inexhaustible, and that its gradual analysis and theory and above all its successive practical application, experimentation, acceptance or rejection, and unfolding, confer and call forth poignant dramatic freshness and inexhaustible uniqueness upon and within every human life, unto the end of time.

ME 1, p. 73

There are certain other ideals and best achievements of certain institutions, which essentially transcend the character, standard and instruments of the Naturally Good. The deepest of the Jewish Psalms, the Seer whose vision of the Suffering Servant of Jehovah is incorporated in the Book of Isaiah, the serenely self-oblivious prayer of Stephen, the deacon, for his enemies whilst they stone him to death; above all, Christ's entire life and work, crowned by the forgiveness of His crucifiers even as He hangs upon the Cross, are the great and the greatest, the most fully explicit, instances of the Supernaturally Good. But indeed, off and on, here and there, sooner or later, we can find, within the larger human groups and during the longer human periods, some lives, some acts, not all different to those acts and lives—at least some touches, some desires for some such lives and some such acts. And if such acts or desires never and nowhere occurred within an entire race of men or within an entire age of the world, then that race and that age would, already by this alone, stand revealed as less than what man actually is—a being natural in his constitution yet variously solicited and sustained by supernatural influences, requirements, helps and aims. The Christian Church, at all times in its indestructible ideal, and indeed always in its fullest and fairest fruits, has been and abides the special training ground, home, and inspirer of this supernatural spirit. Our Lord's Beatitudes are its classical expression, and the Feast of All Saints is the perennially touching commemoration of its countless manifestations in every age, clime, race, and religious environment.

EA, pp. 199–200

Heaven is not a necessary environment for not cheating in the sale of peas or potatoes, for not smashing street lamps, for not telling calumnies against one's wife or brother. But only Heaven furnishes the adequate environment for the elevation and expansion of spirit of a Damien, when he, here below, devoted himself to sure leprosy for the sake of his outcast fellow-creatures; of a Joan of Arc, when, in the France of her day, she reaped her short earthly success and her swiftly following witch's death; or of the average trooper on the *Birkenhead* going down, without moving, at attention, with the women and children being saved alive before his eyes in those boats where he was deliberately refusing to take a place at the cost of others, many of whom had no special claim upon himself. Indeed all of us have ourselves witnessed, or have learnt from eye-witnesses, deeds or dispositions of a similar quality. Humanity will never, universally or permanently, treat such acts as folly, or indeed as anything less than the very flower of life. Yet to claim that the Trades Union, or a Political or Social Party, or the State, should or could, or ever wisely will, require such things, or directly work for them, is assuredly quixotic. Such a demand or hope can only lead to a dangerous Utopia, followed by a not less dangerous reaction. Thus such heroic goodness points to a Beyond, as indeed does all philosophical research, all scientific work, all artistic effort—whensoever these endeavours penetrate deeper than a certain superficial and conventional level. All such heroic, self-oblivious search and reception of Truth and Beauty, as possessing the right to such self-surrender, appear as special divine gifts rather than as mere human efforts, as glimpses of realities which, for their adequate environment and apprehension, require, not this world and this life, but another life and another world.

EA, pp. 200–201

With regard to specially precious manifestations of the experience and conviction of Eternal Life, of God with man, within the authoritative Institutions, in these our times, we can again point to ... deep spirituality and heroism in the Roman Catholic Church. The present writer's mind dwells ever specially upon four examples.

There is the rough uncultured Belgian, Father Damien, deliberately contracting and dying the loathsome, slow death of a leper, from love of God in men utterly without claims of any other kind upon him, away in an island lost in the ocean at the Antipodes, as Robert Louis Stevenson has unforgettably described the simple, splendid life.

And there is, again, Jean Baptiste Vianney, the now beatified simple peasant Curé of Ars. How impressive are the accounts by the Abbé Monnin, an eye-witness of the Curé's utter absorption in God and in souls, each ever inciting the other, and the joyous expansion of his entire nature through this keen sense and love! And in the *Spirit of the Curé d'Ars*, chronicled by the same, we find numberless deeply spontaneous sayings, such as the following: 'Time never seems long in prayer. I know not whether we can even wish for heaven!' Yet 'the fish swimming in a little rivulet is well off, because it is in its element; but it is still better in the sea.' 'When we pray, we should open our heart to God, like a fish when it sees the wave coming.' 'Do you see, my children, except God, nothing is solid—nothing, nothing! If it is life, it passes away; if it is fortune, it crumbles away; if it is health it is destroyed; if it is reputation, it is attacked. We are scattered like the wind.' 'You say it is hard to suffer? No, it is easy; it is happiness. Only we must love while we suffer, and suffer whilst we love. On the way of the cross, you see, my children, only the first step is painful. Our greatest cross is the fear of crosses' (pp. 28, 40, 114 Eng. Trans.).

And then there is Eugénie Smet, the daughter of a burgher of Lille (1825–1871), who, as Mère Marie de la Providence, founded an Order of devoted women, at work, even before her death, as far as India and China; who insisted upon remaining in Paris throughout the siege and the Commune, 1870–71; and who slowly died there, in agonies of cancer, utterly absorbed with joy in God, the Eternal and utterly Real, and with tender and unceasing activity towards His poor and sick around her. In the midst of these immense trials she was wont to say; 'Let us feel that Eternity is begun; whatever pain we are going through, let us make joy out of that thought.' And: 'In all things I can only see God alone; and, after all, that is the only way to be happy. If once we begin to look at secondary causes, there is an end of peace.' (Lady Georgiana Fullerton, *Life of Mère Marie de la Providence*, 4th ed., 1904, pp. 241, 237)

And finally, there is before my mind, with all the vividness resulting from direct personal intercourse and deep spiritual obligations, the figure of the Abbé Huvelin, who died only in 1910. In the *Conference on some of the Spiritual Guides of the Seventeenth Century*, Abbé Huvelin says of Père Condren: 'He has hardly written any books; he wrote in souls'; 'he experienced greater inner derelictions and strange obscurities—a man is not called to form other souls without having to suffer much'; and 'his call was not to live for himself, but to live utterly for Him who gave him all things.'

In speaking of M. Olier, M. Huvelin exclaims: 'Strip yourself of self, love God, love men; what are all these other things that seem of such importance to you?' And he declares: 'The world sees, in this or that soul, the passions, the bitter waters which fill it; but we priests, we seek, beneath these bitter waters, the spring of sweet waters, Arethusa, that little thread of grace, which, though deeper down and more hidden, is nevertheless most truly there.' And again: 'The true means to attract a soul, is not to attenuate Christian doctrine, but to present it in its full force, because then we present it in its beauty. For beauty is one of the proofs of truth.'

As to Saint Vincent de Paul, he tells us : 'See the reason why, in this life so devoted to his fellow-creatures, you will find something austere, and shut up in God : it is that the Saint feels the necessity, for himself and for others, thus to re-immerse, to temper anew his soul in the source of all love.'

And lastly, with respect to the great Trappist Abbé de Rancé, he observes : 'When something very high and inaccessible is put before human nature it feels itself impelled to attain to that height, by something mysterious and divine which God infuses into the soul.' And : 'There is ever something mysterious in every conversion; we never succeed in fully understanding even our own'; nevertheless, 'the voice of God does not speak in moments of exaltation. Such converted souls would say : "It was in the hour when I was most mistress of myself, most recollected, least agitated, that I heard the voice of God." '

Thus souls, who live an heroic spiritual life within great religious traditions and institutions, attain to a rare volume and vividness of religious insight, conviction, and reality. They can, at their best, train other souls, who are not all unworthy of such training, to a depth and tenderness of full and joyous union with God, the Eternal, which utterly surpasses, not only in quantity but in quality, what we can and do find amongst souls outside all such Institutions, or not directly taught by souls trained within such traditions. And thus we find here, more clearly than in any philosopher as such, that Eternal Life consists in the most real of relations between the most living of realities—the human spirit and the Eternal Spirit, God; and in the keen sense of His Perfection, Simultaneity and Prevenience, as against our imperfection, successiveness and dependence. And we find that this sense is awakened in, and with, the various levels of our nature; in society as well as in solitude; by things as well as by persons. In such souls, then, we catch the clearest glimpses of what, for man even here below, can be and is Eternal Life.

EL, pp. 371–378

A good simple, yet somewhat dry and conventional Roman Catholic priest, a worker for many years among souls, told me one day, in a South of England town, of the sudden revelation of heights and depths of holiness that had just enveloped and enlarged his head and heart. He had been called, a few nights before, to a small pot-house in the outskirts of this largely fashionable town. And there, in a dreary little garret, lay, stricken down with sudden double pneumonia, an Irish young woman, twenty-eight years of age, doomed to die within an hour or two. A large fringe covered her forehead, and all the other externals were those of an average barmaid who had, at a public bar, served half-tipsy, coarsely-joking men, for some ten years or more. And she was still full of physical energy—of the physical craving for physical existence. Yet, as soon as she began to pour out her last and general confession, my informant felt, so he told me, a lively impulse to arise and to cast himself on the ground before her. For there, in her intention, lay one of the simple, strong, sweet saints of God at his feet. She told him how deeply she desired to become as pure as possible for this grand grace, this glorious privilege, so full of peace, of now abandoning her still young, vividly pulsing life, of placing it utterly within the hands of the God, of the Christ whom she loved so much, and who loved her so much more; that this great gift, she humbly felt, would bring the grace of its full acceptance with it, and might help her to aid, with God and Christ, the souls she loved so truly, the souls He loved so far more deeply than ever she herself could love them. And she died soon after in a perfect rapture of joy—in a joy overflowing, utterly sweetening all the mighty bitter floods of her pain. Now *that* is Supernatural.

EA, pp. 223–224

And as to heroic watchfulness and accuracy with regard to natural facts apparently of no religious import whatsoever, there is the impressive death of the Jesuit astronomer, Father Perry, sent by the British Government, as head of one of the expeditions, to the South Seas, for the observation of the transit of Venus. Perry, shortly before the transit, was seized by a fever which would surely promptly kill him. He thereupon quietly made his preparations for death and received the last Sacraments, and then absorbed himself, as though in perfect health, in the transit. From the first moment to the last he took and registered all the manifold delicate observations with flawless accuracy. And then, immediately the little planet had ceased all junction with the great resplendent sun, the hero astronomer gently fell back into unconsciousness and death.

EA, p. 289

... An Irish Roman Catholic washerwoman with whom I had the honour of worshipping some thirty years ago in our English Midlands ... had twelve children, whom she managed to bring up most carefully, and a drunkard husband, an Englishman of no religion, openly unfaithful to herself. The constant standing of many years at last brought on some grave internal complications: a most delicate operation would alone save her life. Whilst resting in hospital against the coming ordeal, with the experts thoroughly hopeful of success, a visiting surgeon came round, really the worse for drink, and insisted with trembling hands upon an examination then and there. This doomed the patient to a certain death, which duly came a week later. Yet from the first moment of the fatal change to the last instant of her consciousness (so the priest who attended her throughout declared to me after all was over) she was absorbed in seeking to respond, with all she was, to this great grace of God, this opportunity of utter self-abandonment to Him, and this although she dearly loved her children, and although she knew well that her eyes would hardly be closed before their father would marry a bad woman and give her full authority over this, their mother's darling little flock. All possible plans were made by the dying woman for each of the children, and from the first moment she spontaneously exacted from the priest a promise to prevent any prosecution of the fuddled surgeon—she never stopped to consider his offence even to forgive it; it was God, and the utter trust in Him, and in the wisdom, the love of His Will, that swallowed up all the pain, physical and mental, and all possible conflicts and perplexities.

EA, pp. 289–290

Captain Horace de Vere ... had recovered from his wounds in the Crimean War, and was back in England in full health, a most happily married man, and the father of two little girls. He continued his military profession and deep interest in his men. He had instituted a small fund from which the troopers of his company were to receive a little extra pay for any week throughout which they had remained sober. One of these troopers nursed feelings of revenge against the Captain, since this officer could not honestly do otherwise than pass the man over for many weeks in succession. At last, on parade one day, the trooper shot the Captain through the back and lungs; but the doomed officer lingered on for a fortnight. Even now the trooper's vindictiveness was not assuaged, and, although he knew well that execution awaited him if the Captain died, he nevertheless persisted in open expressions of hope that his officer would die. But de Vere, after providing for his young wife and little girls, concentrated all the strength that remained to him to win his murderer's forgiveness, and to soften that poor hate-blinded heart. And he succeeded: the Captain died fully resigning into God's hands the wife and children and his own life, still well on the upward grade. He lost his bodily life, but he gained a soul: he went to God assuredly a saint, the meek, self-less victor in a struggle between malignant hate and perfect love.

EA, pp. 287–288

Spiritual Joy, Beatitude, does not, indeed, always accompany or crown in this life even high heroism, although I believe this non-flowering of heroism to be always caused by some inhibitory influence distinct from the heroism as such. Yet Spiritual Joy, Beatitude, does appear in the very greatest, the most super-natural, acts and lives. Thus with our Lord Himself, we have the great rejoicing in the spirit during the Galilean ministry; and if the last act of His Life appeared to be the cry upon the Cross, we have to remember that the specifically Christian conception of Jesus Christ absolutely requires, not only the sufferings of the Passion, but also the Beatitude of the Risen Life; neither alone, but only the two, the bitter sweet together form here the adequate object of our Christian faith ... Catherine Fiesca Adorna, that unhappily married, immensely sensitive, naturally melancholy and self-absorbed woman, who ended, as the Saint of Genoa, on the note of joy and of overwhelming joy; and, above all, the Poverello, St. Francis of Assisi, who next to Our Lord Himself, appears, amidst all the Saints we know of, to have most completely brought out the marvellous paradox of Christianity—utter self-donation with entire spontaneity, a hero-ism quite unrigorist, a devotedness of supreme expansiveness and joy.

EA, pp. 290–291

For it means high heroism, yet also hospitable homeliness, it means the Alpine Uplands—the edelweiss and the alpenrose—as well as the Lombard Plains with their corn and their potatoes; it means poetry and prose, a mighty harmony and a little melody, or rather it means, taken as a complete whole, a great organ recital, with the *grand jeu* stop of Supernature drawn out full and all the pipes of Nature responding in tones each necessary in its proper place, yet each sweeter and richer than its own simply natural self.

EA, p. 284

Chapter IX

A CONCLUDING NOSEGAY OF THE
WISDOM OF BARON VON HÜGEL

I AM very glad you are again visiting the poor people—am sure you have real gifts that way. I have always much regretted that my deafness has so crippled me in that direction. I feel as if it would have done me much good, even though I am not sure whether I would have had gifts that way.

    LTN, p. 107

(Of Fénelon's *Letters*)If God, if Christ, loves men—and who can doubt it?—He loves the *average* very much—the poor little virtue, the poor little insight. How splendidly Fénelon feels in her a certain unchristian aristocraticalness of mind—she was evidently a sort of Dean Inge in petticoats. Mind, Sweet, you bathe in, you saturate yourself with, those letters!

    LTN, p. 108

And there was my ever great, rich, heroic *Abbé Huvelin*. It is true he was 72 when he died last summer. But then *what* a suffering in life for 40 years and more, and what a spiritually joyous, *what a faithful* life.

    B. p. 261

The following ten advices given by Abbé Huvelin to von Hügel, May 26–31, 1886, are here translated from the French:
    Prayer will be for you rather a state than a precise and deliberate act.
    The truth is for you a luminous point that tapers off little by little into obscurity.
    (Speaking of the Scholastics and of their way of presenting religious abstractions) But as for me, I cling to the realities; they,

they have the formulae. It completely escapes them that life, all life, eludes analysis. What they dissect is a dead cadaver. It is a trifling business. Pass them by with a gentle, a very gentle smile.

Detachment ought never to be practised for itself. I detach myself only in order to attach myself. I let go the evil or the less good in order to seize the better or the perfect. But I never let go in order to fall into a hole.

Let others make you suffer; never inflict suffering on others.

There is no security in critical work; prayer avoids obstinacy, that's all.

It is only by means of the part of truth which they have that souls really live. Love this truth in them, and them in developing it—and they will end by eliminating error.

Yes, it is necessary to act. You are ill. The activity will therefore have in its nature something repulsive to you. But have no fear: act, love; you have an infinite need for expansion; constraint will kill you.

You can always do a great deal of good by opening yourself to persons who are receptive to you. You will convince them that they are not completely alone in the world.

Our Lord won the world, not by his fine speeches, by the Sermon on the Mount, but by His blood, by His suffering on the cross.

SL, pp. 58–62

As well insist to Kepler on the duty carefully to consider the stars, or to Darwin on his obligation minutely to watch the fertilization of orchids, or to Monica on her guilt if she does not love Augustine: as to preach responsibility for belief to a soul full of the love and of the joy of God.

EA, p. 18

To sanctify is the biggest thing out.

LTN, p. viii

Be silent about great things; let them grow inside you. Never discuss them: discussion is so limiting and distracting. It makes things grow smaller. You think you swallow things when they ought to swallow you. Before all greatness, be silent—in art, in music, in religion: silence.

LTN, pp. ix–x

I want to prepare you, to organise you, for life, for illness, crisis and death. Live all you can—as complete and full a life as you can find—do as much as you can for others. Read, work, enjoy— love and help as many souls—do all this. Yes—but remember: Be alone, be remote, be away from the world, be desolate. Then you will be near God!

LTN, pp. xi–xii

Do not be greedy of consolation. I never got anything that way. Suffering teaches: life teaches. Don't weaken love; never violate it. Love and joy are your way. Be very humble, it's the only thing. That is why I try to keep my little thing always on her knees.

LTN, p. xvi

A religious woman is often so tiresome, so unbalanced and ex- cessive. She bores everyone, she has no historical sense. I want to teach you through history. History is an enlargement of per- sonal experience, history pressing the past. We must have the closest contact with the past. How poor and thin a thing is all purely personal religion! Is there any such thing as a purely original thinker? You must get a larger experience—you gain it by a study of history; the individualistic basis simply doesn't work.

LTN, p. xiv

Dullness, dreariness and loneliness. East winds always blow- ing; desolation, with certain lucid intervals and dim assurances. Be always faithful. You will find you would rather lose life it- self than this life. *Après tout*, the last act in life is devotion— devotion in death. I like that.

LTN, p. xvi

Never try to begin to help people, or influence them, till they ask, but wait for them.

LTN, p. xxix

The power of evil in a world ruled by an omnipotent God the source of all good; we never get rid of this problem. We can only minimize it. There are people who pretend that the earth- quake at Tokio was a good thing—to have cancer in the face is somehow splendid, and shows the goodness of God! I hate all that talk. Evil is a mystery, and you don't do away with it by calling it good.

LTN, p. xxvi

'A great foot, a pierced foot, prevents that door closing there.'

LTN, p. xxxvi

Religion is dim—in the religious temper there should be a great simplicity, and a certain contentment in dimness. It is a great gift of God to have this temper. God does not make our lives all shipshape, clear and comfortable. Never try to get things too clear. Religion can't be clear. In this mixed-up life there is always an element of unclearness. I believe God wills it so. There is always an element of tragedy. How can it be otherwise if Christianity is our ideal?

LTN, p. xvi

Those who most exalt the power and need of grace do so usually by most depreciating nature. God thus gets glorified in direct proportion as man gets vilified. The more holy I find God, the more wicked I feel myself to be. This is touching and real, and almost irresistible to vehement natures, but it is dangerous and excessive.

LTN, p. xxviii

I hate rigorism—it's all wrong. Our Lord was never a rigorist. He loved publicans and sinners. How He loved all the beauties of nature, the family—children! His parables are full of these homely things. God nearly always teaches us through a person, he teaches us through individuals. Follow his lead. Live from day to day, even from hour to hour. I want you to learn to die to yourself daily; the daily death is a spiritual habit. You want heroism and renunciation—more, you want wisdom and discipline: organise yourself. Perseverance is one of the crowning graces of God. Get rid of all self-occupation. I don't mean self-examination for conscience sake, though that, too, can be over-done. But self-oblivion is a splendid thing; move out of yourself, let in God. Never pray but you realise that you are but one of a countless number of souls, a countless number of stars.

LTN, p. xxiii

The Christian life begins, proceeds and ends with the Given. The Otherness, the Prevenience of God, the one-sided relation between God and man, these constitute the deepest measure and touchstone of all religion.

ME 1, p. xvi

The existence of a personal Reality sufficiently like us to be able to penetrate and move us through and through . . . is the original and persistent cause of this noblest dissatisfaction with anything and all things merely human.

EA, p. 11

And that joy, pang, and expansion is, each and all, in the closest touch with, and is occasioned and sustained by, the experience of Eternal Life—the reality of the Abiding God.

EL, p. xiii

We are not God. Yet how we need Him! And this, then, not as just a larger ourselves, not as a larger Becoming, but as Being, as Joy, Pure and Undefiled.

LTN, p. 136

INDEX